+LC4704.73 .C66 1992

Comfort, Randy Lee, /Teaching the unconv
LC4704.73 .C66 1992 C.1 STACKS 1992

```
LC          Comfort, Randy Lee,
4704.73        1943-
C66            Teaching the
1992           unconventional
               child
```

	DATE DUE		

AUDREY COHEN COLLEGE LIBRARY
345 HUDSON STREET
NEW YORK, NY 10014

Teaching the
Unconventional Child

Teaching the Unconventional Child

Randy Lee Comfort

1992
TEACHER IDEAS PRESS
A Division of
Libraries Unlimited, Inc.
Englewood, Colorado

*This book is dedicated to the many children
who have allowed me to learn with them,
and to Dr. Mel Levine,
who taught me how to do the learning.*

*... warmth and gratitude to Roxanne Torke
and Ron Ritchhart:
special friends, magical teachers.*

Copyright © 1992 Libraries Unlimited, Inc.
All Rights Reserved
Printed in the United States of America

No part of this publication may be reproduced, stored in a retrieval system, or transmitted, in any form or by any means, electronic, mechanical, photocopying, recording, or otherwise, without the prior written permission of the publisher. An exception is made for individual library media specialists and teachers who may make copies of activity sheets for classroom use in a single school. Other portions of the book (up to 15 pages) may be copied for in-service programs or other educational programs in a single school.

TEACHER IDEAS PRESS
A Division of
Libraries Unlimited, Inc.
P.O. Box 6633
Englewood, CO 80155-6633

Library of Congress Cataloging-in-Publication Data

Comfort, Randy Lee, 1943-
    Teaching the unconventional child / Randy Lee Comfort.
    xi, 162 p. 17x25 cm.
    Includes bibliographical references and index.
    ISBN 0-87287-941-0
    1. Learning disabled children--Education--United States.
2. Special education--United States. 3. Remedial teaching--United States. I. Title.
LC4704.73.C66 1992
371.9'0973--dc20   92-10118
                                                              CIP

Contents

Preface ix

1 – THE UNCONVENTIONAL CHILD......................... 1
    Defining Learning Disabilities................................ 2
    Recognizing the Unconventional Child........................ 5
    Summary of Strategies...................................... 10
    Reference List.. 11

2 – THE LEARNING PROCESS.............................. 12
    Input.. 13
        Visual Perception...................................... 14
        Auditory Perception................................... 14
        Sensory Perception.................................... 15
        Social Perception..................................... 16
    Processing and Remembering............................... 16
    Output.. 19
    Summary of Strategies...................................... 20
    Reference List.. 21

3 – DEVELOPMENTAL DIFFERENCES....................... 22
    Learning Deficits... 23
    Cognition.. 24
    Temperament.. 25
    Social-Emotional Development 27

v

3 – DEVELOPMENTAL DIFFERENCES (*continued*)
- Behavior 29
- Summary of Strategies 32
- Reference List 32

4 – STRATEGIES FOR TEACHING AND LEARNING 34
- The Caring Classroom 34
- How Children Learn 38
- Behavior Management 42
- Accommodating for Differences 44
- Good Strategies for All Teachers 50
- Reference List 51

5 – TEACHING AND LEARNING TO READ AND WRITE 54
- Language Communication 55
- Strategies for Accommodating Specific Weaknesses 66
  - Visual-Spatial Organization 66
  - Sequencing 67
  - Language Processing 68
- General Strategies for the Slower Learner 70
- A Scenario 71
- Summary: Identifying or Recognizing Language Dysfunctions ...75
- Reference List 77

6 – TEACHING AND LEARNING MATHEMATICS 78
- The Concept of Numeracy 79
- Specific Examples of Teaching Strategies 92
- Summary: Recognizing and Attending to Mathematical Dysfunctions 97
- Reference List 99

7 – PARENTS AND TEACHERS TOGETHER 101
- The Uncertainty of Learning Difficulties 101
- Reference List 108

8 – GENERAL ACCOMMODATIONS AND ADAPTATIONS FOR CLASSROOM TEACHERS 109
- Adapting Classrooms to Meet Individual Needs 111
- Summary of General Accommodations 121
- Reference List 121

Appendix A	Resources Relating to Social-Emotional Issues and Friendships	123
Appendix B	Resources for the Language Arts	125
Appendix C	Resources for Mathematics	129
Appendix D	Resources for Parents and Teachers	133
Appendix E	General Resource and Reference Information	137

Bibliography 141

Index 155

About the Author 162

Preface

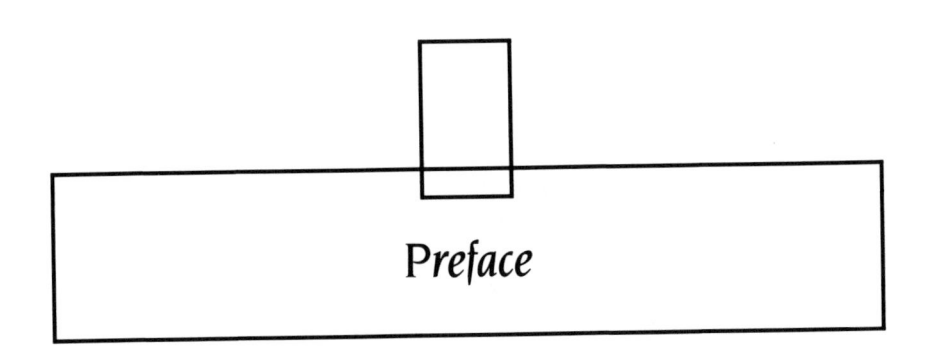

In 1980, I wrote *The Unconventional Child*, a book for parents of children with learning difficulties. Subsequently, it was suggested that I should have included "living difficulties." That is an omission that I would like to rectify in this new book, because many children who struggle in school have a troublesome time in their family and social environments as well. Many parents, teachers, and other professionals then asked if I would write a similar book for teachers of unconventional students. It has taken me twelve years to learn enough to feel that I could make a viable effort in that regard. *Teaching the Unconventional Child* is the result of over twenty years of parenting, counseling, teaching, and learning experiences.

The national trend in this decade is to integrate children of various learning styles into regular classrooms, but many teachers feel inadequately prepared to meet the educational, emotional, and behavioral needs of children who learn and live differently. Teachers, like parents, of unconventional children will find themselves frustrated and exhausted, especially if they are operating without the understanding and the skills they need to work effectively with students who have trouble in school. *Teaching the Unconventional Child* will help teachers know how and what accommodations can be made in the classroom that will facilitate progress. The book is designed to augment a teacher's understanding of the life of children with various learning dysfunctions and to make educational adjustments that can enhance the learning process.

Teachers will see that *patience* and *endurance* are words that take on new meanings as they become involved with increasing numbers of students who have difficulty learning information they need for academic and social functioning. Similarly, creativity and imagination are concepts whose potential becomes unlimited when teachers work with more and more students who have learning deficits and unusual processing or temperamental styles.

Teaching the Unconventional Child is not a recipe book. It would be presumptuous to suggest that there are definitive answers to the very complicated and sensitive problems experienced by children who manifest learning and living difficulties. However, certain strategies have been particularly successful, and various classroom accommodations do seem to work well in many cases. The strategies presented suggest both a place to start and a means of carrying on from there. The strategies offer a way to approach children who learn differently, and they conceptualize ideas for teaching "in a different voice" (Gilligan 1982). These techniques and ideas have emerged as corrections of mistakes as well as from the wonderful "ah-ha!" experiences of success. The suggestions come from teachers, parents, counselors, and, most importantly, from the students themselves.

It is my hope that readers of this book will feel challenged to try some of these teaching techniques and classroom accommodations; that they will build on them, contest them, and create new and viable alternatives. The book is not one of answers; rather, it provides ideas, suggestions, resources, and techniques that are based on contemporary research, on a broad base of experience, and on trial and error. It is a guide to understanding children who have difficulty in school, and it is written with practicality and do-ability in mind. The book should help teachers to generate their own thoughts for creatively designing teaching strategies that can help children to learn. *Teaching the Unconventional Child* will stimulate teachers to think imaginatively and respectfully, and it will inspire reciprocity in the teaching/learning process. The goal of *Teaching the Unconventional Child* is one of learning—learning to learn—which, ultimately, is much more exciting than knowing.

Teaching the Unconventional Child is designed from the general to the specific so that the book begins with a broad description of the unconventional child and the ways a teacher might identify and think about the student who is learning and behaving differently. The second chapter deals with the process of learning itself, because knowing how learning occurs is relevant to understanding how individuals may vary within that process. In the third chapter, developmental differences are discussed because cognitive, temperamental, social-emotional, and behavioral development is not even within any given child, or from child to child. These aspects of development play an important role in the student's readiness for school, both academically and socially.

Actual teaching strategies, while indirectly presented throughout the first three chapters, are described and spelled out beginning in chapter 4. A variety of alternatives are presented so that a teacher can design an educational and behavioral program that will be appropriate for the child in question. Chapters 5 and 6 are an elaboration and an extension of the previous chapter in that strategies especially for reading, writing, and math are offered. Both of these chapters conclude with specific examples of lessons that might work well in most classrooms.

Chapter 7 is a brief description of how parents of unconventional children often feel and react. Suggestions of how parents and teachers can work together and approach the educational process as partners are presented in this chapter.

The book concludes with some overall accommodations and adaptations that many teachers will find broad enough to apply to a variety of classroom situations, yet specific enough to help them deal with individual needs and styles.

The appendixes are designed to augment and enhance the theoretical and practical ideas and concepts that have been presented in each chapter. Both literary references and names of organizations and national resources have been included so that teachers and parents can utilize materials and groups that are known to be helpful in working with children who learn and live unconventionally.

1

The Unconventional Child

Usually I am unpredictable, but sometimes, just to surprise everybody, I do exactly what is expected of me.
— Anonymous

As I walked into the room, I noticed Debby slipping farther down into her chair, putting on the leave-me-alone face I later came to know so well. Debby's teacher had asked me to come in to observe her class because she was confused by the inconsistencies of this student. Yesterday Debby had written her name perfectly well and had completed all of her math problems flawlessly. Usually Debby reversed the **b**'s and sometimes the **y** in her name. Her math work was frequently full of number reversals. Debby's teacher did not know whether Debby was "lazy and inattentive" or if there were some learning difficulties for which this six-year-old student needed some additional help. In the ensuing months, I learned from Debby that she tried hard most of the time, but sometimes things came out okay, and sometimes they did not. She never knew why she was successful when she was, and she could never predict whether or not she would be the following day. Despite good cognitive ability, Debby's school work was hampered by specific visual and motor difficulties. She was having trouble learning to read, and she could not copy from the board or from workbooks consistently because she reversed many letters and numbers, often putting them in the wrong order or in the wrong columns.

Only a first grader, Debby already was learning that school was an unhappy place to be.

Teachers have a difficult time knowing what to do about children who seem to be learning or behaving differently. It is difficult to judge whether a particular child's difficulties have to do with a specific learning dysfunction, or whether it is a question of maturity and development. Nevertheless, the teacher who is an astute observer can play a vital role by describing how the child behaves and learns in the classroom. Especially with young children, accurate, detailed descriptive stories can be even more valuable than are the standardized tests and the categorical labels that "experts" may assign to the child.

DEFINING LEARNING DISABILITIES

The term *learning disabilities* (LD) was first introduced in 1963 by Samuel Kirk. Unfortunately, developing a definition for the term has presented an unconquerable challenge, with each new definition having certain shortcomings. The federal definition was proposed in August 1975, in the form of Public Law 94-142 (Education for All Handicapped Children Act of 1975) and reads:

> Specific learning disability means a disorder in one or more of the basic psychological processes involved in understanding or in using language spoken or written, which may manifest itself in an imperfect ability to listen, think, speak, read, write, spell, or to do mathematical calculations. The term includes such conditions as perceptual handicaps, brain injury, minimal brain dysfunction, dyslexia, and developmental aphasia.

A learning disorder, as defined by the Learning Disabilities Association Membership Services Committee (1990, p. 3), "affects the manner in which an individual with normal or above average intelligence takes in, retains, and expresses information." The Learning Disabilities Association proposes that many LD children will fail in school unless their disabilities are discovered and diagnosed properly, "enabling them to receive assistance in educational, medical, psychological, and social services" (p. 3).

Various educational and medical groups stand by other definitions, although most seem to agree that learning disabilities include neurological dysfunctions, uneven growth patterns, academic difficulties, and a discrepancy between potential and achievement. Julian Haber (1989) describes LD as "a disorder in which the individual's brain handles information in a way that blocks learning" (p. 162). Sally Smith (1987) states that a "learning disabled child is a child with a disorder ... and that disorder is the key characteristic of these children ... " (pp. 1 and 3). Mel Levine (1987) prefers to talk about "developmental variation," encouraging clinicians, educators, and researchers to describe essential elements of a child's developmental function and performance (p. 7).

In the long run, of course, a precise definition does not ameliorate the problem. One might do equally well by focusing on the titles of the many books that have been written to describe the home lives and classrooms of children with learning differences. Clearly, such titles come from the hearts of parents: *The Difficult Child*, Turecki (1985); *Can't Read, Can't Write, Can't Talk Too Good Either*, Clark (1974); *No Easy Answers*, Smith (1987); *Something's Wrong with My Child*, Brutten (1979).

Public Law 94-142, mainstreaming, individual education plans, resource rooms, and various other means of serving LD children have been developed to attend to students with special needs, but these are all highly controversial programs and ones which have caused tremendous conflict concerning the use of labels for children, the monies to be spent on programming, the rights of parents, and the appropriate educational plans for young students. There is very little agreement among parents themselves, let alone between families and schools, as to what an "appropriate" education is and how it might be acquired.

As an expansion of and follow up to Public Law 94-142, Public Law 99-455 (Education of the Handicapped Act Amendments) was passed in 1986. These amendments provided for attention to the newborn child, with specific intervention being made available to babies from zero to three years. In the last half of the 1980s, therefore, most federal funding was designated to support programs that addressed the first three years of life. Although it is crucially important to provide intervention at this early level, the result of these funding priorities left little money available to aid educators and other professionals who work with preschoolers and early elementary school students who have learning difficulties.

According to Public Law 94-142 and Public Law 99-455, the child must be served in the "least restrictive environment," which, for children from zero to three years, is in the home. For preschoolers, however, the least restrictive environment implies a group setting with nonhandicapped children. An appropriate education in the "least restrictive environment" for the early school-age child with learning dysfunctions, as mentioned earlier, is not easily defined or provided. One of the biggest challenges for teachers is how to offer the best individualized instruction for a child with a learning disability.

Learning disability has become a trendy label carrying a high price tag. Some buy this designer fashion in order to acquire special services for children who learn and behave differently, while others shun the product

4 ■ THE UNCONVENTIONAL CHILD

precisely because of the label. Since teachers and parents often are at a loss as to how to help some children who have school and behavior difficulties, it may feel safer to put a label of explanation on these youngsters. Once we know that a child has cerebral palsy, for instance, it explains why the child cannot do certain things—or at least we think that it does. Labeling a learning disability may feel more comfortable for some parents or teachers.

Eileen Senior (1986), writing about children who are developmentally young, questions whether kindergarten and early elementary school-age youngsters who develop more slowly are "learning disabled or merely mislabeled" (p. 161). Similarly, Jill Rachlin (1989) asks whether learning disabilities are a medical fact or a "convenient fiction used to label away problem kids" (p. 60). Both of these articles, and many more, suggest that untraditional methods of teaching could offer an approach to learning that would benefit far greater numbers of students in every classroom. While few would deny that improved teaching would be an asset, many educators, physicians, and mental health professionals stand firmly in contending that true learning disorders do exist.

An accurate definition of LD is less important than the practicalities of how to help children learn. For the most part, "unconventional" children or children with "learning differences" will be used instead of LD throughout this book. Unconventional children are those who do not live or learn as do the majority of their peers. Most teaching is directed toward that majority, however, so youngsters who are exceptionally bright in various areas, or students who learn differently in certain arenas, may not have their individual needs met for part or most of their academic day.

> Martin is a second grader who is just beginning to manifest reading difficulties. Described as an energetic, athletic boy in kindergarten and first grade, he also seemed to do quite well academically. Now, in the second grade, his teacher notices that he can read sight words accurately, but he cannot seem to put the words together when they are in sentences. Martin is not successful with sequences of words or numbers. An educational evaluation that included a sensory-motor assessment indicated that Martin is a child who deals best with material that is presented kinesthetically (tangible, concrete, hands-on materials with which he can be involved physically). In kindergarten and first grade, Martin did well because there were many manipulatives involved in his learning process. Sight word reading was not problematic because he could learn a single word, often making a concrete picture association with it. Sequential material presented more difficulties, however, and fewer hands-on

materials were being used in his second-grade classroom. It was observed that Martin was very good in gymnastics and in karate, even though a number of sequential steps were involved. Evidently, the physical involvement of his body, the actual doing of the task, helped Martin to solidify the processes involved in learning the material. Martin will need a lot of physical input in his school learning.

Learning outside the "norm" may mean that a child with variant learning behaviors has less access to the content of what is being taught in any given classroom. While some youngsters may reside consistently within the parameters of the norm throughout their school day, many others vary from class to class, so that a child may take in effectively what is offered in math and science but may incorporate little language arts instruction. A child who rarely understands oral directions in reading class may do well in history where the teacher outlines and writes down everything to be studied. It is not unusual for extremely bright children to experience learning difficulties in one or more areas; but, like Debby, their cognitive abilities often go undetected because their performance is so poor. Alternatively, a child may not be academically astute but may be quite brilliant musically, socially, or athletically (Gardner 1983).

Teachers who are hired by public schools probably fit within the expected norm of the public school system that hires them. Similarly, private school teachers need to fit within the parameters of the school's philosophy or else they will not be hired. Children, however, are not hired for school—especially for public school. The student may be more at odds with the system than the teacher, and teachers may be more alike than students are.

RECOGNIZING THE UNCONVENTIONAL CHILD

Variation in learning style is a reflection of the human brain—and neither learning style nor the human brain is perfect. Some learning and behavioral styles, however, are more conducive than others to school success. The student who reads well but cannot sing is better off than the child who dances beautifully but cannot spell. However, one does less well if one is talented mechanically but not mathematically, if one is energetic not quiet, or if one is creative not conforming. The child who needs his own space, demands unusual structure, misinterprets directions, and perceives a world differently than most age-peers offers a challenge to teachers and parents that is not easily met. It is important to remember that a multitude of history's most eminent personalities were individuals whose unconventional behaviors and learning styles led them to inventiveness, creativity, athletic prowess, social responsibility, and significant discovery that far exceeded their more conventional schoolmates. Galileo, Charles Darwin, Thomas Edison, Vincent Van Gogh, Ernest Hemingway, and Franklin Roosevelt were all brilliant leaders in their fields who experienced significant learning difficulties.

Although most parents (usually mothers) know that their child is different by three, four, or five years of age, official identification rarely occurs prior to school entry. By kindergarten, however, some children with variant learning styles are already beginning to "fail" because they cannot meet the challenges that schools require of them. The demands of the school system are a puzzle to them, and they cannot manage outside of their protected home environment, which is often geared to meet their particular needs.

Some children may manifest symptoms of disabilities in the preschool years, but noteworthy characteristics may not be observed until first or second grade. Moreover, unconventional children often have excellent compensatory skills and may manage to move through early elementary school "masking" their difficulties, with more severe deficits not emerging until fourth or fifth grade when the "pressure begins." The older elementary student is required to perform certain tasks in specified ways and at particular times. As the student's deficits become increasingly difficult to hide, the student's poor performance becomes more noticeable. This is the child who performed adequately in preschool and kindergarten, tolerable in first, second, and third grades, but problematically in the fourth and fifth grades. The dysfunction was always there, but it was tendered by good faith, good intellect, good family support, and less academic stress.

A third-grade teacher tells me about Peter, whose amazing memory and fund of general knowledge masked his inability to read. In the second grade, Peter could recite *Tom Sawyer* word-for-word after hearing it two or three times. He seemingly "read" many second-grade books (which he had actually heard other children read and then memorized them), and he certainly understood everything that was read to him. These skills focused attention away from his reading problems, which only became apparent in third grade when Peter was required to read books on his own and to write book reports on the books he had read.

If basic learning deficits go undetected and unremediated for too long, a child's self-esteem is likely to suffer because *the child* is aware of not keeping up with peers. Few children have learning problems without having some degree of emotional overlay as well. Many students having learning differences develop emotional vulnerabilities as secondary symptoms. Delayed maturation or learning differences can result in a perception of self as a continual failure academically, athletically, or socially. Unfortunately, "difference" is not understood or valued in most schools, and schools are not as child-centered and respectful of individuality as we would like to think they are. Teachers and administrators cannot afford to permit tremendous latitude and must require a certain amount of conformity. Deviation in behavior or learning style can be accommodated only to a point.

As opposed to physical handicaps, "hidden handicaps" are less discernible so it is possible for children with learning dysfunctions to go undiagnosed, or misdiagnosed, for many years. In the early grades, for example, most of the expectations center around auditory processing and verbal information. Students are asked to follow directions, listen to stories, sing songs, and cooperate in group activities. A child who is socially adept and who has good listening and talking skills will thrive in this environment. Occasionally there may be a teacher comment that Jayne does not care much for the art corner, that she rarely plays with puzzles, Legos®, or markers. Essentially, though, this is not seen as a red flag since Jayne has adapted well to preschool. By kindergarten, it may be noted that Jayne "doesn't seem to have mastered cutting with scissors as yet." Again, this would not be considered reason for major concern. Jayne behaves; she has friends; she participates during circle hour; and she loves story time.

> In the first grade, the teacher observes that "Jayne seems to be having a bit of trouble with learning to print her letters and numbers." Jayne, being the particularly social and bright child that she is, manages to avoid penmanship by making frequent trips to the drinking fountain, and then to the bathroom, by offering to be the class messenger who will run the notices down to the office, by taking the role of narrator rather than recorder during cooperative learning activities. By the fourth grade, Jayne's teacher phones her parents to report that she never turns in her book reports, that her math papers are extremely sloppy, and that she is very lazy about attending to written assignments.

This is not an unusual example of how a child with specific hidden handicaps can slip easily through the cracks. Standardized testing would find Jayne verbally precocious and overall well within the range of above-average intelligence. She probably would not qualify for specific services because her verbal performance scores, particularly at age nine, are not "bad" enough and do not show a two-year discrepancy. A learning specialist would note specific educational difficulties, which are not motivational or emotional, although certainly these factors are involved by fourth grade as secondary symptoms. Jayne's handwriting and fine motor skills need attention and remediation; yet, it is easy to appreciate how these weaknesses were overlooked in the early years, before the school curricula demanded much in the way of writing.

Another child may be identified more readily early on because weaknesses surface as problems as soon as the child enters school. Children experiencing auditory processing delays and sensory integration deficits frequently present themselves as behavior problems from day one at school. In fact, their very attention-eliciting behaviors enable them to receive the early intervention they need. This is to their advantage. As an example, statistics reveal that seven of ten children with learning difficulties are boys. Actually, it may be that boys bring attention to themselves more readily than do girls because boys generally tend to be more active, energetic, outspoken, and aggressive. The well-behaved, quiet, socially skilled youngsters (often girls) may go unnoticed. In early school years, it is usually unconventional *behavior* more than any specific *educational* deficit that invites intervention. Even girls who are diagnosed early are most often referred because their behavior is dysynchronous. By definition, a diagnosed learning disability cannot occur in preschool since a diagnosis requires a discrepancy between tested intelligence and academic achievement (of which there is none in preschool); but certainly one can detect a predisposition to future learning problems. Rarely, and rightfully, is a kindergarten child referred because he is reversing letters or because she cannot sing on tune, or because she "holds her pencil funny." For some, these anomalies are stages. For others, they are not.

It is the combination—the pattern, the conglomeration—of behaviors and skills which a teacher or parent needs to observe. For instance, a teacher might recognize that a child in the class seems unable to perform many tasks commonly assigned to age-peers. This child not only cannot cut with scissors in kindergarten, but the child also is unable to color within the lines, match shapes and sizes, fit pegs into holes, or serve snacks without spilling. The youngster may not put puzzles together, do dot-to-dot designs, or hold a crayon for more than a minute or two. If the child does not keep up with any of the children in nearly every area, there may be a developmental delay, and the child could be considered as "overplaced" in kindergarten. If, however, the student appears to be cognitively astute, is able to communicate ideas, and can relate what is being learned in one area to another but falls behind in specific skill areas, one might suspect that the child has a learning dysfunction and would benefit from an assessment.

Teachers of young children are aware of the wide variety of behaviors displayed by perfectly "normal" well-developed children as they sit and work in classrooms, play and socialize in school, cooperate and argue on the playground. Symptoms of learning differences and developmental variations, therefore, are not easily identified. As one comes to place less emphasis on the identification of a disability, however, and more energy on observing specific behaviors, it becomes increasingly possible to recognize which children are in need of additional attention and in what areas they require help. Some teachers find it useful to carry a clipboard or notebook to write down their observations as they move around the classroom. Many find that writing helps them to be more attentive and accurate observers. Someone might complain that a particular child "always speaks out of turn," but when counting the actual number of times this occurs in an hour, an observer may find that the child only spoke out of turn three times.

As a further example, many youngsters who experience no specific learning difficulties are impulsive and haphazard about their work. Children with short-term memory deficits often are impulsive students also. They speak out without raising their hands, they talk or act before they are called upon, they rush ahead with an activity the minute the first direction is given (not waiting for all the directions)—because they are afraid they will forget. They cannot remember long enough to wait, so they do not wait; they just act. This symptom (impulsivity) in the hurried, careless student and in the short-term memory-deficit student is the same; yet, the treatment of each is different. A full, comprehensive description of the specific behaviors of each child leads to appropriate instruction.

Teachers and parents spend an enormous amount of time with children. They are the most reliable providers of descriptive information, and they have the most comprehensive perspective of a child in the numerous realms of everyday life. A youngster in a diagnostician's office is rarely the same child seen by teachers and parents, who experience the student in large classrooms, in social settings, and in structured and unstructured environments. Many students with learning deficits behave gloriously well on a one-to-one basis with an adult in a quiet office, where all or most of the adult's attention is directed toward the child; yet, this same youngster may be horrendously dysfunctional in a busy family or in an action-oriented classroom setting.

Similarly, a child may be able to manage well with an adult who is likely to overlook certain unconventional behaviors; whereas, interpersonal relationships with less tolerant peers may be troublesome. For example, it is not unusual for children who see and hear differently in the classroom to take in social information differently as well. Language-based deficits are frequently intermingled with peer relationship problems. Again, teachers are in a good position to observe a child's friendships, social interactions, feelings of self-worth, and sense of independence. Descriptive observations from teachers and parents are vitally important in the multidiagnostic process of assessment, and the importance of a multidiagnostic evaluation cannot be overemphasized. It often happens that a child who is referred to a specialist for an assessment will reflect a difficulty pertinent to the particular specialist: psychiatrists see psychiatric problems; speech and language therapists recognize linguistic difficulties; educational consultants pick up on academic weaknesses. Similarly, many school evaluations are guided by the financial, political, or adjunct resources that dictate the school's policies and regulations.

To be served best, a child needs the input of many descriptive narratives. A broad vision of a whole child will identify unique strengths, weaknesses, styles, and interests. Tidy labels will not work for characterizing or for remediating the difficulties, nor for enhancing the strengths of a child.

SUMMARY OF STRATEGIES

IF	THEN
The parent has called or come in to talk about the child	Watch to see if you observe the same child as the parent does.
You find yourself continuously aware of, speaking to, or watching a child	Start recording behaviors. How often and for what reasons are you in touch with this child?
You notice a child stands out, withdraws, or acts differently from most others	Describe the behavior. What exactly is the child doing? When?
The child seems to be avoiding certain activities or overemphasizing other activities	Make a concerted effort to involve the child in the avoided activity and observe the outcomes. What does the child do when the overemphasized activity is not available?
A child's behavior is difficult for the teacher	Observe whether the child gets positive or negative feedback from peers.

REFERENCE LIST

Brutten, Milton, Sylvia O. Richardson, and Charles Mangel. (1979) *Something's Wrong with My Child*. San Diego: Harcourt Brace Jovanovich Publishers.

Clark, Louise. (1974) *Can't Read, Can't Write, Can't Talk Too Good Either*. New York: Penguin Books.

Gardner, Howard. (1983) *Frames of Mind*. New York: Basic Books.

Haber, Julian, M.D., and Florence Issacs. (1989) "Helping Learning Disabled Children." *Good Housekeeping* 209, no. 3: 162.

Kirk, S. (1963) Behavioral diagnosis and remediation of learning disabilities. Paper presented at Conference on the Exploration into the Problems of the Perceptually Handicapped Child: Evanston, IL.

Learning Disabilities Association Membership Services Committee. (1990) Position paper by National Joint Committee on Learning Disabilities, Washington, DC.

Levine, Melvin. (1987) *Developmental Variation and Learning Disabilities*. Cambridge, MA: Educators Publishing Service.

Rachlin, Jill. (1989) "Labeling Away Problem Kids: Are Learning Disabilities a Medical Fact or a Convenient Fiction?" *U.S. News & World Report* 106, no. 3: 59.

Senior, Eileen M. (1986) Learning disabled or merely mislabeled? The plight of the developmentally young child. *Childhood Education* 62, no. 3: 161-65.

Smith, Sally. (1987) *No Easy Answers: The Learning Disabled Child*. New York: Bantam Books.

Turecki, Stanley, and Leslie Tonner. (1985) *The Difficult Child*. New York: Bantam Books.

2

The Learning Process

When asked what learning was the most necessary, he said: "Not to unlearn what you have learned."
—Diogenes Laertius, 200 A.D.

Margaret looked at me when I asked her to draw a picture of herself doing something she liked to do. Then she looked at the blank paper in front of her. After a while she looked at the colored markers. She sat back in her chair and let her eyes roam around the room. I thought she might be picturing herself in various activities that she would want to draw, so I gave her another minute.

Suddenly, Margaret turned to me and said, "I forgot what you said."

I asked if she remembered any part of what I had said, and she replied that she was supposed to draw a picture, but she didn't know of what. I repeated, " ... of you ..." at which point, she impulsively picked up a marker and started making a circle for her head.

"Wait," I said softly. "Let's remember all of it. I would like you to be doing something in the picture. Can you think of what you would like to be doing?"

"Playing?"

"I don't know. Do you like to play? I would like you to draw you doing something that is fun for you; something you like to do."

"I like to play checkers with my mother," Margaret said.

"Good," I responded. "Can you draw a picture of you playing checkers?"

Margaret, eight years old, began to draw. As she did so, she became more and more involved in the picture, and she began to tell me a very elaborate story about the last time she and her mother played checkers. What usually takes a child somewhere between five and fifteen minutes to do in an initial session with me, took Margaret well over half an hour. At that, I stopped her before she was really finished.

Cognitively, Margaret matches Brazelton's (1969) description of the slow-to-warm-up child: the child who takes longer to size up the situation, to amass all of its pieces in a comfortable fit, and to make a good response to the demands of the situation. Margaret has some difficulties with processing. She has trouble with starting because she retrieves and organizes information slowly, even though all of the information is there and she can understand it.

In the sense that a pumpkin in the patch is not the same as pumpkin pie on the table, the existence of information does not mean that one has the information, or that having the information means that one can use it. Arriving at pumpkin pie requires a process of selecting, assimilating, and utilizing various ingredients. Similarly, in order to be knowledgeable one must be able to deal with information in certain meaningful ways.

Although there are many elaborate neurological, developmental, and pedagogical theories explaining how learning takes place, most incorporate a paradigm in which data are 1) taken in, 2) processed, 3) remembered, and 4) put out. There are variations on this theme, but input, processing, and output are the essence of what "knowing" is all about. Children who have trouble with learning and knowing in certain areas usually are experiencing a gap or a breakdown in this pattern of acquiring, integrating, and expressing information.

INPUT

In order to take in information, one must be able to see it, hear it, and/or feel it in a meaningful way. It is not just vision, hearing, and tactile sensitivity that are involved. It is also the visual, auditory, and kinesthetic perception of the stimuli. Children with learning difficulties may see with 20/20 vision, but they may not perceive "rightly" (Saint Exupery 1943). Some children may perceive straight lines to be wobbly; they may not be able to discriminate the C from the G tone on the piano. What smells good to one person may be offensive to another. How one takes in any particular stimulus is important to how one will treat the stimulus once it has been ingested.

Visual Perception

Perception of visual designs is an important skill in a modern literate society because there is constant demand to read and to discriminate among visual data. Reading, for instance, requires the visual perceptual capacity to recognize parts and wholes, spatial relationships, figure-ground differences, and object constancy. The figure of vases and faces is a common example of individual visual perceptual variations in that some people see "vases" first while others see "faces" first. With continued attention, the vases and faces usually reverse themselves in the eyes of the beholder. All of that can be fun and interesting until one realizes that for people having certain perceptual difficulties, reading is a similar "game" in which the reader may sometimes see black on white and other times white on black. In reading, however, it does not work if one sees white shapes on a black background. Moreover, if letters are reversed or turned upside down, the perceived word cannot be decoded or identified.

Whole-part perceptual difficulties can cause many confusions. Focusing on visual details may be necessary and important in some instances, while it is detrimental in others. To remember (recognize) a person's face, one cannot see only the eyes (part). Rather, the whole (all of the face) must be taken into account. On the other hand, recognition of most individual words (parts) on a page (whole) is essential for successful reading.

How one perceives the world visually has vast implications for daily living. It has been suggested that many artists see the world differently from the average person, which may be a part of what contributes to their creative success. However, many of the visually creative artists find themselves to be dysfunctional in the more practical, everyday world in which visual creativity can become problematic. There are both social and pragmatic implications that result from visual perceptual variations.

Auditory Perception

In the well-known children's game of Telephone, children delight in whispering a word or phrase around the circle and coming up with an entirely different word or phrase at the end of the line. For five-year-old

Arthur, however, the experience of interpreting words incorrectly every day is an exasperating way of life. His kindergarten teacher asks the class a question. Amy nudges him, and says, "You have to know!" Arthur is puzzled: "Half my toe?" This makes no sense to him, and he asks her to repeat what she said. The teacher scolds Arthur for talking, and tells him to pay attention! Arthur's mother has noticed that Arthur frequently misses what is being said, and she wonders if he has a hearing problem, but the physician has found no hearing loss, and assures Arthur's mother that many five-year-old boys do not pay much attention to what their parents or teachers say to them. The doctor is sure that Arthur will "outgrow" this soon.

The ability to recognize what is said is different from hearing. Just as one must differentiate parts and wholes and shapes of black on white in visual perception, so one must be able to discriminate between background and foreground stimuli auditorily, and one must be able to separate salient sounds (words) from incidental noise (traffic or air conditioning) in conversations. Phonemes need to be differentiated and letter blends must be recognized.

The classroom setting is a difficult environment for children who have trouble with auditory discrimination. The many and varied stimuli encourage distractibility and inattention for those who are hypersensitive to sound, are easily confused auditorily, or for those who do not know which auditory stimuli are the important ones on which to focus.

Sensory Perception

Most school tasks demand touch and body movement as part of information gathering. Social relationships are heavily dependent upon one's sensitivity to physical place and being. As preschool children sit in circle-time, they learn to respect their neighbor's sense of space. Two children may be happy sitting close to one another, holding hands, overlapping legs; while two others may fight over who is in whose place, or who touched whom. As they move through junior high and crowded halls, one child can tolerate the bumping and jostling, while another has the sense that "other kids are always hitting me." One little person in preschool cannot stand wearing shoes; another refuses to walk barefoot. Children who do not like to be touched or who must always be touching, tend to have trouble in groups, messy activities, or art projects. Those who have a poor sense of balance or those who are unclear about where they are in space are often those who have trouble adjusting to the school bus ride, group projects, physical education activities, and risks or dares.

Social Perception

The seeing, hearing, and feeling of social cues is now recognized as being an important factor in child development. Hypersensitive youngsters may "over-read" social interactions, attaching more importance to a word or gesture than was actually meant. What most children will ignore or move beyond, the overly sensitive child clings to with undue intensity.

At the other end, poor social readers never take in the cues at all or, at best, they "under-read" them. They are oblivious to body language, verbal nuance, or group moods. What everyone else just feels or knows is elusive for them. They end up saying, "Nobody told me," or "I didn't know." Somehow, it is never their fault.

Social perception has been framed linguistically within the visual, auditory, and tactile modalities. That is to say, when an argument occurs between two children, a teacher may say to each child, "How did you *see* what just happened?" After the children reply, the teacher may respond, "I'm *hearing* you say..." and then the teacher may add, "I wonder how you are *feeling* about this situation?" In other words, we use seeing/hearing/feeling words to describe what occurs socially because we do not have social words; yet, social perception is important in school and in everyday learning, and contributes to one's adaptability and emotional well-being.

PROCESSING AND REMEMBERING

> He remembered that he had been remembering something. He had been right on the edge of it ... but it was something a long time ago, and there was a strangeness about it, something bothersome and a little scary, and it hurt his head the way it hurt his head sometimes to do arithmetical sums without pencil and paper. When you did them in your head something went round and round, and you had to keep looking inside to make sure you didn't lose sight of the figures that were pasted up there somewhere, and if you did it very long at a time you got a sick headache out of it. That was what remembering was like a while ago, but he hadn't been able to see what he knew was there.
> — Wallace Stegner

Once information has been taken in, something needs to happen to it. In making a milkshake, we put ingredients into the blender. Nothing will happen to them unless we activate the blender. Similarly, the child at school must be able to do something with the incoming information. Levine (1987) suggests that most stimuli "arrive for processing packaged either in a simultaneous array or in a specific serial order" (p. 68), and that an effective learner in school needs to be able to deal with both packages.

Simultaneous and sequential processing are not unlike the whole/part situations discussed earlier. Simultaneous processing is concerned with the perception of a gestalt, while successive or sequential processing is concerned with a temporal order of a series of elements. Both are necessary for efficient acquisition of educational material.

Whether the information is taken in simultaneously (all at once) or sequentially (one thing and then another), it has to be managed in a coherent and meaningful fashion once it arrives. Again, individuals rely on their own particular strengths for dealing with incoming information. For the visually adept, mind-pictures will be made and stored. Those who depend upon auditory strengths will make internal tapes which can be shelved and replayed. Certain people who have tactile sensitivities will say that they associated particular words with feelings. A seven-year-old boy said, "I like the word cozy because it feels good."

How one processes and stores information is an individual and organizational preference, but it is not entirely volitional. People who are especially organized seem to have an internal department store of well-compartmentalized information. As the information shipment arrives, various items are separated and slotted into particular brain sections. A five-year-old who was talking about how he knows things related that "You put things in different folders in your brain, and then when you want something, you go to that folder." The blender-oriented individuals may be able to stash a large amount of information all together. This is called *chunking*.

Some information is stored associatively, which means that seeing or hearing one part reminds one of a related part; hearing the name Elvis Presley makes one think of rock and roll music; seeing a soldier in a combat uniform associates the soldier with war. Other information may be processed according to categories. We put bananas in the fruit category, shoes in with clothes, and cat in with animals. Sometimes information is processed and remembered in links or chains, where one thing leads to the next and serves as a kind of cuing. Examples for young children are activities such as getting dressed, responding to fire drills, or learning a song. Older children may need to remember the steps necessary for doing long division, attending a movie or sports event, or baking a cake. Certain material is remembered by rules: red lights mean stop; i comes before e except after c; shower before entering the pool. School days and certain academic fields (math and science) tend to have many rules to remember.

Processing information means making sense of incoming material and holding onto it in a form which enables one to retrieve it. It is possible to take in and understand information without remembering it, however. Many of us do this with jokes we hear. We understand the joke, but we forget it before it can be recalled for retelling. Similarly, it is possible to remember something that is not understood. In learning to speak Portuguese in an initial Peace Corps training session, the instructor repeated a certain phrase until each of the students could recite it flawlessly. For an entire week, they remembered and recited this phrase without having any idea (understanding) of what it meant. The best learning takes place, however, when there is understanding and remembering together. It is usually easier to remember something if it is understood.

Maintaining information is dependent upon memory, which is often thought of as an independent system; but, in fact, it is not. There is no discrete central nervous system center identified as memory. Although there are several medical conditions which are predisposing to memory difficulties, most children experiencing memory dysfunctions do so as a result of inefficient wiring (Levine 1990).

Every student must deal with the challenge of remembering information since retaining academic material, accessing important and relevant facts, and generalizing acquired data all depend on memory. On the menu of memory, there are short-term or long-term memory, active memory, working memory, and retrieval memory. A. R. Luria, in *The Mind of a Mnemonist*, and Oliver Sacks, in *The Man Who Mistook His Wife for a Hat*, have written exquisite clinical tales depicting the magnificent distortions which can result from memory sensitivity and memory loss.

Accumulating and holding onto information are essential processes for learning to take place. On the other hand, William James commented that if we remembered everything, we should be as ill as if we remembered nothing. He was speaking metaphorically about social relationships and personal integrity, but his statement also addresses the practical importance of not cluttering our minds with unnecessary information. The eight-year-old's parents who comment "He has a phenomenal memory because he remembers minute details of things which happened and places we went in the past" may find that this same child cannot remember to write down homework assignments or to bring his gym clothes to school. He may not remember what his teacher said 10 minutes ago when she gave the math instructions, and he may not remember if he is supposed to wait for his mother after school or go home on the bus. He would be better off "forgetting" having honey on his biscuits at the Clover Cafe five years ago when visiting Grandma, so that he could have room in his memory for the more important information coming in each day at home and in school. At the very least, this information should be moved from short-term to long-term memory so that it will not get in the way of his current functioning and learning.

OUTPUT

Once material has been taken in, assimilated, and stored, it must then be available for retrieval and output. Some children know certain information but have trouble making it available. They cannot recall a particular word they want to use, or they see a picture of a thermometer and know what it is, but cannot name it. They may recognize the correct spelling of a word if they see it written, but cannot retrieve the right letters in the right order for spelling it on their own. Other children may have access to the information, but may lack an appropriate vehicle for disseminating it. This could be the child who has excellent language comprehension, but poor language expression. The child has the thoughts and ideas, but cannot say them. Another child may be able to say the words, but cannot write them because of poor motor skills. For example, the child could spell "house" but could not write it because motor planning or the mechanics of writing are too difficult.

One is very limited in social interchanges, in intellectual relationships, in athletic endeavors, if the output roads are blocked off. A preschooler, for instance, is heavily dependent upon oral communication for "fitting in," for making friends, for getting needs met, for participating in the classroom. Kindergartners and early elementary school-age children need verbal-expressive skills as they are often called upon to "show and tell." The middle elementary school child is required to express ideas in written work. Book reports, journals, and stories are important parts of second, third, and fourth graders' school lives. Motor planning and motor output are important tools needed for the accomplishment of these tasks. Both gross and fine motor abilities enable students to negotiate seat-work, to move about the classroom, to pass in the halls, and to play at recess. They are important in the myriad athletic, artistic, dramatic, and vocational ventures of all students. Children with significant output difficulties are limited in their abilities to communicate in meaningful ways both socially and educationally. Mutuality is an important feature in relationships whether they may be the dialogue of friendships or the didactic interchange in academia.

In the extreme, the British scientist Stephen Hawking is a poignant example of how output dysfunction can be devastating. Here is a brilliant scientist whose mind gloriously assimilates and synthesizes enormously complex material that he seemingly ingests and processes with relative ease; yet, that mind remains alone and noncontributory because there is no capacity for output. Dr. Hawking's cohorts have gone to incredible lengths to facilitate the unleashing of these thoughts and ideas so that the information can become accessible to others.

Except for these extreme cases, and including the blind and the deaf, information gathering and producing is usually a multisensory process, even though one facet may be stronger or weaker than another in any given individual. Even so, gaining and using knowledge cannot be reduced to an easy three-step formula because each of these processes can be enhanced or impaired by extenuating influences. Attentional attributes, temperament, socio-economic status, cultural heritage, motor functioning, and self-esteem are powerful contributors to the total learning process.

SUMMARY OF STRATEGIES

IF	THEN
A child seems confused, lost, unfocused, disruptive, or withdrawn	Think in terms of processing deficits, not just emotional difficulties.
A child does well most of the day, but is not "getting" material which is visually oriented	Do some individual work which focuses on directionality, on letter/number recognition, puzzle assembly, or design. Have a chat with parents: "This is what I'm noticing. Do you see it at home, too?"
A child does well in most areas but not with verbal instructions	Do individual auditory tasks which include understanding one-on-one and which involve phonetic distinctions.
A child seems unduly awkward, is always touching someone or something, will never sit or stand close to anyone, and will not put shoes or sweaters on or take them off	Think in terms of tactile and sensory integration weaknesses. Describe behaviors; request OT/PT evaluation.
A student is consistently alone, is rarely chosen to be a partner, is seldom included in group activities, is frequently in tears or tattling, or is overreactive/underreactive	Talk with the child about school and friends. Learn about how the child perceives his/her situation. (Does it differ from your perception?)

IF	THEN
A child seems to understand information but has trouble remembering it	Observe the student for memory deficits: What kind of information is remembered and when?
A child seems to understand at the time, but does not use the information	The student may be having trouble with processing information. Note specific examples as they will be important for assessment purposes.
A student gives back information or shares knowledge verbally but not in written form	Think about fine motor abilities and motor planning.
A student gives back information in written form but not verbally	The student may have language-based difficulties.

REFERENCE LIST

Boslough, John. (1985) *Stephen Hawking's Universe*. New York: Quill/William Morrow.

Brazelton, T. Berry. (1969) *Infants and Mothers*. New York: Dell Publishing.

Levine, Melvin. (1987) *Developmental Variation and Learning Disabilities*. Cambridge, MA: Educators Publishing Service.

———. (1990) *Keeping a Head in School*. Cambridge, MA: Educators Publishing Service.

Luria, A. R. (1987) *The Mind of a Mnemonist*. Cambridge, MA: Harvard University Press.

Sacks, Oliver. (1987) *The Man Who Mistook His Wife for a Hat*. New York: Harper & Row.

Saint Exupery, Antoine de. (1943) *The Little Prince*. New York: Harcourt Brace & World.

Stegner, Wallace. (1990) *Two Rivers*. In: *Collected Stories of Wallace Stegner*. New York: Random House.

3

Developmental Differences

All I can say, doctor, is that the boy never got anything congenital from my side of the family.
—Medical News Tribune

It is not surprising that we misunderstand one another; rather it is amazing that we ever understand one another.
—Doreen Kronick

"If he is as brilliant in math as you say," laments the third-grade classroom teacher to the teacher of gifted-math, "you would think he could write his book report with a correct sentence or two in it. His spelling is atrocious, and I'm not even sure I believe that he read the book!"

These two teachers have trouble recognizing the same student. Robin is, indeed, phenomenally astute with numbers and number concepts. He looks at a wall and sizes up the number of bricks it took to construct it. He watches a plane in the sky, and imagines how far it can go in how much time. He sits down to dinner and estimates the number of Rs in his alphabet soup; but Robin reads slowly and laboriously, because the letters keep moving around the page, and the lines go in waves for him. He has trouble writing the letters, too, many of which turn out backwards or upside down. He cannot think of the right word to use, and then when he does, he cannot spell that word, so he has to think up another one.

Robin would rather do math. Numbers make sense to him; words are too confusing!

LEARNING DEFICITS

One of the most difficult concepts for teachers and parents to internalize is that very bright individuals can and do have learning deficits. We understand that a healthy child can have a broken leg, but we have trouble accepting that an intelligent youngster can have a language dysfunction, a writing problem, or a reading disorder. "If the child is so smart," says the teacher, "why can't he understand that he has to follow the directions I gave in class?" Intellectually, the child does know that he is supposed to follow the directions, but he may not know what the instructions are. The ability to organize, to sequence, or to process auditorily a series of directions is not correlated to intellect. There is not a cause-and-effect relationship between cognitive capacity and functional deficiency.

It is probably useful to enter into one of the numerous "games" people play in order to learn about what it feels like to have a learning disorder. The following reading tasks serve to increase one's empathy for the student who experiences visual perceptual dysfunctions:

IMAGINEHOWCONFUSINGITWOULDBEIF
EVERYTHINGYOUREADLOOKEDLIKETHIS!

ORIFTH EWOR DSBE GINA NDEN DI NPLAC ESTH
ATDON'TM AKES ENSET OY OU?

TAHW FI EHT SRETTEL EREW DESREVER or
OTU FO ODRER?

Now imagine being called on to read aloud and the   w   o   e   o

r s e t

ds   m

d   n   e a l   e h   c

a   l   o   r   l   e.

c   v   e p a

People can wear a Walkman® headset turned to a fairly loud volume while trying to talk on the telephone if they want to sample the life of a child with auditory screening difficulties. Try writing with your non-dominant hand for a minor motor-output deficit, or with your toes for a significant motor impairment. Memorize a poem in a foreign language, perhaps a language with a different alphabet, in order to experience memory difficulties. Think about listening to a long lecture on a topic about which you have no interest or prior knowledge when it is exceedingly hot and you are thirsty. Do you think you might acquire an attention deficit?

Your success or failure in the above exercises has nothing to do with your intellectual ability. These are circumstances that could arise for any individual at any time, and ones that require unusual energy and concentration for management. For the student with a specific functional disorder, it is not a one-time exercise, but a way of life — a life that comes to be frustrating, exhausting, emotionally wearing, and sometimes debilitating.

Understanding the way a child learns and recognizing the student's strengths and weaknesses are crucially important to the further development of the student's academic, social-emotional, and behavioral achievement. The value of a multidiagnostic assessment is that the whole child can be taken into account. Cognition, temperament, emotionality, and behavior are all a part of the child, and they must all be considered as a package in formulating a comprehensive educational program for the child. Interestingly, most teachers do this almost subconsciously, on an informal basis, for each student in class. A visitor coming into a preschool classroom might be told that Sarah brings her own snack because she does not like graham crackers; that Todd only wears blue shirts; that Mona likes story hour, but never plays with clay, paints, or anything messy. The teacher may have observed that Brent has many friends and socializes easily, while Alex seems to incite trouble the minute he sets foot on the playground.

These kinds of behavioral observations are integrally important to teaching because knowing a child and a child's particular sensitivities and styles will enable the teacher to present material in a way which will help a child to learn and to grow. It is the interaction of cognition, temperament, and social/emotional/behavioral style in each child which needs to be taken into account in planning an educational program which works.

COGNITION

Cognition (intellect, inherent ability) is sometimes remarkably obvious, but most often it is not. Cognition is concerned with the ability to think. It is how people take in, organize, retrieve, and use various kinds of information. Cognitive abilities can continue to develop at all life stages, but a disturbance in the processes of thinking can impede an individual's developmental growth, and can spill into emotional and behavioral development as well.

Reuven Feuerstein (1980), a noted Israeli psychologist and educator, has encouraging data which indicate that cognitive ability is not static, and that it can be dramatically expanded under proper learning conditions. This suggests that many students experiencing one or more low-severity handicaps could improve their overall intellectual functioning if helped to develop efficient learning strategies. Without intervention, however, large numbers of bright students remain intellectually laggard and passive throughout their educational careers.

The vast majority of children with learning difficulties have average or above-average intellectual ability which means that cognitive capacity is usually not the primary issue. In fact, more often than not, adequate intellect is what hinders children from getting the specific help they need because it is assumed that they are "smart enough" to do the work if they try harder. Kim Reid (1990) has rightly pointed out that these children need to be taught to try "smarter" not "harder." A child with visual motor output deficits could be very bright without its having any effect on her penmanship. She could try over and over to make the letters correctly, but if her perception of the letters is erratic or unpredictable, it will not matter how much or how long she tries. She needs to be taught specific strategies for making the letters so that they are guaranteed to go the right way, and she needs to be taught to keyboard on a word processor. Given these adjuncts to supplement the learning process, the child is able to try "smarter."

TEMPERAMENT

"Temperament is the natural, inborn style of behavior of each individual" (Turecki 1985, p. 13). In 1956, Chess and Thomas introduced the idea of temperamental differences as a quality *belonging* to the baby, not *given* to the baby: "...we found that temperamental qualities could be distinguished in children from early infancy on, and that these qualities had their own effects upon parents and others" (Turecki 1985, preface). In turn, of course, interactional feelings and responses evolve with the baby molding the environment as well as vice versa.

The temperamentally difficult child, as described by Chess and Thomas (1983), is one who experiences irregularity in biological functions. As an infant, the baby may have had trouble with body regulation—couldn't eat, sleep, or wake up with any regularity. Neurologically, the sensory-motor functions of integration and organization may not have been developed well enough to enable the infant to deal with or adapt to the demands of the environment. A child who is hypo- or hypersensitive to any kind of stimulation is often one who also is temperamentally volatile. The infant who experiences these kinds of temperamental frailties is thus likely to be the one who is stressed quickly by environmental demands, such as the need to integrate and to organize internal and external stimuli. In writing about the "growth-promoting environment," Greenspan (1981, p. 24) contends that caretakers may find themselves significantly challenged when faced with an infant who is difficult to comfort. Therefore, the less-adaptive child, the one whose constitutional differences impede normal development, may experience relationship disturbances. Emde, et al. (1982) concur, pointing out that the baby's behavior elicits a particular caregiving response, and may exact considerable patience from the caretaker to react sensitively to a child who fails to develop age-appropriate behavioral and emotional responses.

There is the suggestion that children with allergies may have more temperamental and learning vulnerabilities than those without allergies. Shyness also has been researched in terms of its correlations with temperament and with difficulties in reading social cues (Caspi, et al. 1987 and 1988). (See appendix A for bibliography on social-emotional development and friendships.)

In looking at temperament and learning style, Holt (1989) suggested that the child who learns quickly has an adventurous nature, runs with risks, and approaches life with openness. On a continuum, the less successful student, says Holt, finds the world to be tricky and senseless. This student does not know what to expect and is not trusting. The youngsters who have a history of constitutional vulnerability, developmental delay, or temperamental dysynchrony seem to be the ones who are poor risk-takers, unpredictable behaviorally, and less likely to experience academic achievement.

Temperamental propensities are quickly noted by every new parent. Mothers refer to "easy babies," "sleepless infants," or "difficult children." "Nothing bothers this child," says one mother, while another bemoans the irritability and crankiness of her newborn. As this mother reads more information, she discovers that the child who is hard to nurture and who has difficulty as an infant will continue to be vulnerable as the child grows older. In spite of the kind of attention received, this child is likely to be difficult to rear throughout childhood and adolescence.

SOCIAL-EMOTIONAL DEVELOPMENT

Children's friendships are important. In *No One to Play With*, Osman (1989) points out that having a friend means having someone to be with and to share with. A friend is someone with whom to cooperate and someone with whom to experience relationships which are different from those provided by one's family. Although most early school-age children have at least one good friend, psychologists estimate that between 5 percent and 10 percent of children in elementary school classes are entirely without friends (Asher 1981; Chance 1989). A child without friends is at risk for failure and is more likely to drop out of school, become delinquent, indulge in criminal behavior, or to suffer from mental illness during his adult life, says Chance (1989). Berndt (1989) concurs and adds: "Problems in friendships and problems in school are not independent ... (furthermore) ... positive peer relationships can have a supportive impact so that students with intimate friendships feel good about themselves and they perform at a high level in school achievement" (p. 34).

An important experience which often is lacking for unconventional children is socialization, or friendship interaction. The learning disabled child has more than educational problems because the same difficulties that interfere with academics are likely to interfere with emotional and social development. Other children tend to surpass the developmentally delayed child in emotional maturity as well as in educational growth. In the first grade, for example, an unconventional youngster may still be working on preschool issues of individuation and separation, while his peers have already resolved or completed that stage of development, and have moved on to issues involving cooperative interaction. The immaturity of the delayed child may make his teachers and peers impatient and angry with the child. Then, as each new academic and social task occurs, it is accompanied by further stress and strain for the unconventional youngster, and the child retreats to earlier behaviors even more intensely than the child might otherwise do.

Larry Silver (1984) points out that "It is essential to distinguish between a child whose emotional problems are causing school and academic difficulties and a child whose emotional problems are the consequences of these difficulties" (p. 58). Emotional problems may have started as a result of developmental delay or learning dysfunction, but if they begin to take on a life of their own, they need individualized attention.

Despite the love and attention of careful parenting, Brad experienced difficulties with internal regulation and external adaptation from the day he was born. At five and one-half years old, he had a tested IQ of 165, sensory-motor integration weaknesses, and significant social-emotional dysfluencies. Brad frustrates easily, and readily falls prey to tantrums. It is difficult to make things "right" for him. His internal unevenness is paralleled by his perception of the external milieu, which he sees as being alternately loving, comforting, and nourishing or insecure, abrasive, and unpredictable. Many of Brad's conversations begin with baby talk. He frequently wears the mask of a clown: a comical, whimsical fellow which is a mockery of all that is requested of him. Brad is the sassy, indignant pedagogue who plays the fool. Verbally astute, intellectually formidable, he mediates his world with words, which becomes wearisome for others and exhausting for him. At the pinnacle of this verbal volcano, he explodes—raging, tumbling. Physically and emotionally out of control, he retreats, and will cry and withdraw for hours. None of this behavior is readily tolerated by adults or peers. Teachers and children are afraid of Brad, who, in turn, is anxious about himself as well.

An absolutely brilliant child, Brad has no specific learning disabilities. He also has no friends—which is a social disability. He does have sensory-motor delays which influence his perception of and response to his internal self and to his external world. Without therapeutic intervention and support, not only for Brad but also for the adults in his life, Brad's developmental course will remain rugged, with his having to negotiate between the cognitive high peaks and the affective low valleys.

A third-grade teacher tells of a little girl who was doing fine academically, but the teacher could not figure out what was going on with this child socially. The girl constantly was lying and stealing from other children. "She just didn't seem to fit into any pattern of anything I knew about," said the teacher, whose curiosity led her to frequent talks with the child. "I had to get her over thinking that she was in trouble," the teacher told me, "so one day I told her that I was just really baffled by what she was doing, and I wondered if she could tell me more about the behaviors she selected." The child all of a sudden popped up with: "It's so exciting when I do these things. Otherwise I'm really bored."

BEHAVIOR

"Jenny, you said your two-times tables perfectly yesterday. I know you can do it today if you'll try."

"If I do well once, then everyone expects me to do well all of the time, and I can't. If I don't do well, there is less hassle, and I don't care if I fail."

Success is sometimes the child's greatest failure. Jenny does not know how or why her times tables came out all right yesterday because there is nothing she knows of which can make her mind work consistently. Every day she tries, but some days the result is correct and some days it is not. Then one day, she gives up and says to herself that it is better not to do it right anyway since she cannot control the results. Jenny becomes quiet and withdrawn in the classroom. To be unnoticed is safe, and to be wrong is safer than being inconsistent.

Adam has trouble with his memory. Although he can remember very specific details of things which occurred when he was much smaller, he can never remember what the teacher just told him to do, or what the school routine is. He has found, however, that the children in his first-grade class think he is very funny when he imitates the teacher behind her back. Adam makes wonderful faces, and is very dramatic. His theatrical abilities bring him instant, consistent, and predictable rewards among his peers. Every adult at school, other than the drama teacher, finds Adam difficult to manage. Adam has been referred for counseling because of behavioral problems. In fact, however, it is Adam's short-term memory difficulties which need to be recognized and addressed.

A fourth-grade child's parents divorced when she was six years old. She lives with her mother, who is a lesbian, and periodically visits with her father, who is a recovering alcoholic. She has been seeing a psychiatrist three times a week for three years. It is assumed that her acting-out, precocious behavior is a manifestation of her unusual family situation. Her fourth-grade teacher, however, has noted that the school reports, dating back to first grade, continuously allude to the child's weaknesses in math and spelling. The teacher alerts the school's learning consultant, who does an assessment and discovers a "sequential organization deficit," meaning that she cannot put things in order, nor can she remember the order — both of which are necessary for math and spelling. Sequential organizational weaknesses often are associated with math and spelling abilities. A closer look reveals that the child does not behave poorly in classes which do not stress these skills, but that she is highly distractible in math class and she is recalcitrant about the rewriting of her very creative compositions.

The above are three examples of the kinds of behavior problems that are frequently symptomatic of learning difficulties, but which often are "diagnosed" as emotional-behavioral disorders. Again, the critical importance of a multidiagnostic assessment is apparent. Behavioral difficulties in early childhood can represent red flags calling for careful attention to learning and sensory-motor delays. Problematic behaviors may be symptomatic of underlying developmental delays or discrepancies. Even adults usually lack the ability to mediate these disorders verbally. Rarely would one encounter an individual who announces, "I behave dysfunctionally because I am covering up for an auditory processing difficulty." However, educational and therapeutic intervention can help to "demystify" a learning deficit, enabling the person to understand it, cope with it, and live with it; so that misbehavior is not the only way to get one's needs met.

As nature and nurture are hard to separate temperamentally, emotions and learning delays are difficult to tear apart behaviorally. Certainly, there are children who do have true emotional disorders which require and benefit from psychiatric intervention. On the other hand, there are youngsters like Adam with temperamental, sensory-motor and/or learning vulnerabilities who develop emotional overlays because living with these deficits is tough to do. Dysynchrony in one's life makes it hard to cope with the demands and expectations of everyday learning and living. This is especially true for those who harbor the hidden handicaps of unidentified learning disorders. Emotional and behavioral dysfluencies often can be mitigated once the weakness is identified, and as it begins to be remediated. Early identification is crucial because educational and therapeutic intervention can prevent long histories of vulnerability.

In 1984, Morrison stated that "There are special needs children in every school. These include the handicapped, the gifted, the children of multicultural heritages, and youngsters with specific learning dysfunctions." In fact, every child has special needs which bid for individualized instruction and attention, and which challenge teachers to be sensitive, observant, structured, and flexible. "Ideally," writes Seligson (1989), "a mandated curriculum should be broad enough to allow teachers to create many of their own plans, but specific enough to provide curricular activities which can supplement the teacher's own ideas." It has been said that a good teacher can make up for a poor curriculum, but never vice versa.

Children who come from multicultural heritages present differences in most American classrooms. Cultural diversity is not a developmental difference, but some children from non-American backgrounds may appear to have learning deficits when they are only manifesting specific ethnic behaviors. Other children who actually do have learning dysfunctions are overlooked because it is assumed that their cultural difference is the reason for their academic difficulty. What appears to be a language or behavioral problem may stem from a difference of cultural expectation and experience, or it may be entirely separate from these influences, and truly reflect a developmental delay. A broader understanding of cultural backgrounds and better information about a child's home life can lead to a more accurate description and diagnosis of a student's functioning.

> A third-grade Puerto Rican boy is in a private school, which is advantageous for developing his very high intellectual abilities. He is a boisterous child, however, who appears immature and demanding of much attention compared to his classroom peers. Frankie rarely completes or turns in homework assignments and seems unusually disorganized throughout the school day. While he is fluent in both Spanish and English, and therefore does not require additional language assistance, it would appear that his attentional difficulties may necessitate outside intervention.
>
> Further investigation, however, reveals that Frankie's mother is deaf, and a single parent of Frankie and two younger children. Every day after school, Frankie must return home to a "second job" in which he makes a series of phone calls for his mother, arranging appointments, negotiating service calls with the electrician, grocer, doctor, and so on, organizing the hearing-world for his family.
>
> When outside help was arranged in order to relieve Frankie of these excessive duties, his school behavior settled down dramatically, and his work was handled more efficiently.

The influences of home, culture, emotions, cognitive abilities, and developmental variations are significant in a child's learning and behavioral growth. To underestimate or to overlook any of these contributors would be a disservice to the child, the family, and the school community.

SUMMARY OF STRATEGIES

IF	THEN
A child is particularly clever in one academic area and very poor in another, but is cognitively bright and astute	There is very likely to be a specific learning disability involved.
A child has a high/low tested IQ score	Little about learning style is known.
A student misbehaves or achieves poorly in school	A diagnostic assessment of educational strengths and weaknesses as well as a psychosocial evaluation should be considered.

REFERENCE LIST

Asher, S., and P. Renshaw. (1981) Children without friends: Social knowledge and social skill training. In: *The Development of Children's Friendships*, Asher & Gottman, eds. New York: Cambridge University Press, 273-96.

Berndt, Thomas. (1989) Quoted by Elizabeth Schultz in "Research." *Teaching and Learning*, 34.

Caspi, Avshalom, Glen H. Elder, Jr., and Daryl J. Bem. (1987) Moving against the world: Life-course patterns of explosive children. *Developmental Psychology* 22: 303-08.

Caspi, Avshalom, Glen H. Elder, Jr., and Daryl J. Bem. (1988) Moving away from the world: Life-course patterns of shy children. *Developmental Psychology* 24, no. 6: 824-31.

Chance, Paul. (1989) "Kids without Friends." *Psychology Today* 23, no. 1 (January/February).

Chess, S., and A. Thomas. (1983 and 1984) *Annual Progress in Child Psychiatry and Child Development*. New York: Brunner/Mazel.

Emde, R., T. Gaensbauer, and R. Harmon. (1982) Using our emotions: Some principles for appraising emotional development and intervention. In: *Developmental Disabilities: Theory, Assessment, and Intervention.* Edited by M. Lewis and I. Tafts. New York: S. P. Medical and Scientific Books.

Feuerstein, R., V. Rand, M. Hoffman, and R. Miller. (1980) *Instrumental Enrichment: An Intervention Program for Cognitive Modifiability.* Baltimore: University Park Press.

Greenspan, Stanley. (1981) *Psychopathology and Adaptation in Infancy and Early Childhood.* New York: International Universities Press.

Holt, John. (1989) *Learning All the Time.* New York: Addison-Wesley Publishing.

Mitchell, Anne, Michelle Seligson, and Fern Marx. (1989) *Early Childhood Programs and the Public Schools.* Boston: Auburn House.

Morrison, George. (1984) *Early Childhood Education Today.* Columbus, OH: Charles E. Merrill Publishing.

Osman, Betty. (1989) *No One to Play With.* Novato, CA: Academic Therapy.

Reid, Kim. (1990) Paper presented at Denver Academy Lecture, Denver, CO.

Silver, Larry. (1984) *The Misunderstood Child.* New York: McGraw-Hill.

Turecki, Stanley, and Leslie Tonner. (1985) *The Difficult Child.* New York: Bantam Books.

4

Strategies for Teaching and Learning

A teacher may teach, but that does not ensure that a child will learn.
—Weiss and Weiss

Teaching does not make learning.
—Holt

Children are always learning. They just may not be learning what we think we are teaching.
—First-grade teacher

When I don't understand the child, I keep asking the child questions. I have to let the child know that there is no judgment and no trouble.
—Third-grade teacher

THE CARING CLASSROOM

The advent of mainstreaming and the change in urban school populations have left many teachers feeling overwhelmed by the extraordinary diversity of children in their classrooms. For the most part, American schools of education have focused on teaching teachers to teach curricula, which becomes increasingly difficult to do in a classroom of 25 to 30 students with varying learning styles. The intent of this chapter is to help teachers learn how to teach children, not lessons, so that the task of helping individual children to construct knowledge becomes less intimidating. Since curricula, regular classrooms, and mainstreaming, in and of themselves, cannot serve to enhance academic learning, social interactions, or appropriate behavior, it is up to teachers to plan for, model, and provide various experiences in which children will have the opportunity to learn.

In the earliest years, being part of a relatively stable group of children and adults is commonly believed to be most beneficial to a child's social-emotional and educational experience. The continuity and stability of the caregiver/teacher contribute to a child's sense of security, which, in turn, enables the child to be available for learning. Research in day care issues (Seligson 1989; Katz 1987; Comfort 1985) consistently affirms that children who form secure relationships with caregivers make smoother transitions between home and school. Mitchell and Seligson (1989) point out that "The essential elements of a secure relationship are the availability and predictability of the teacher" (p. 226). Katz (1987) confirms the importance of the relationship when she talks about the "psychological safety" or the attachment a young child develops for the teacher.

> Young children need adults who accept the authority that is theirs by virtue of their greater experience, knowledge, and wisdom ... (Children) thrive best when they feel loved by someone they can look up to.

Teachers at any grade level who have little or no understanding of early childhood development are at a disadvantage in their classrooms. Knowledge of the various stages of growth and development, some appreciation of Piaget's constructs of a child's ability to acquire and utilize information, and at least an awareness of the psychosocial evolvement of children's emotional behaviors are basic to appropriate educational instruction. Teachers of very young children will be most effective when they incorporate learning through play in their lesson plans, while the teachers of early elementary students will want to remember that learning solidifies most readily when there is active involvement with materials as well as with ideas. Educational planning for all young children must be rooted in the knowledge that a young child's primary modes of learning are language and play. Three-, four-, and five-year-olds like to play with problem-solving materials which represent direct, concrete experiences of their world. The symbolic representation and reconstruction of the child's daily experiences will be played out repetitively. During this time, children also are acquiring social knowledge by recognizing and interacting with a cast of characters who populate their home, school, and community environments.

It is not until later that children are able to engage in more abstract manipulation of cognitive concepts, or in more perspective taking in social situations. The child with developmental delays may lag behind chronological peers in this maturing process, so that in third grade, a given student may look much like a kindergartner or first grader in parts of the student's development. Teachers who are unaware of the early stages of growth and development will experience a "teaching disability" in their attempts to reach this student.

Teachers of young children benefit from providing a dependable, consistent classroom schedule which is geared to a child's total development. Although it has been found that youngsters with variant learning styles do best in highly predictable situations, it is also true that almost all young children benefit from consistency, reliability, and predictability. In fact, many techniques which are specifically taught in special education classrooms actually would contribute to the learning of most children in regular classrooms as well. Sometimes, however, there are exceptions. It is well known that children with attention deficits, for instance, learn and survive most effectively in very small, contained settings in which there are few, if any, detractors. Cruickshank (1961) pointed out that the best classroom for normal children may be the worst classroom for children with an attention deficit because the "appropriate" stimuli of attractive walls covered with student artwork, various activity centers, and colorful educational aids and charts decorating the room are all "inappropriate" to the child with an attention deficit who is so easily distracted and diverted. On the other hand, ADD students, like all young children, do function well in classrooms which offer consistency and predictability.

The caring classroom is one which affords an opportunity for a child to learn with an adult who provides security for every student at whatever level the child may be developmentally. Greenspan (1988) postulates that the normal facilitating experiences provided by most parents and teachers usually are not adequate for the child with a developmental delay because that child requires additional direction and instruction. The 1986 National Association of Education for Young Children (NAEYC) position paper states:

> The teacher's role is to prepare the environment for children to learn through active exploration and interaction with adults, other children, and materials.

It is Greenspan's contention that children with disabilities often fail to develop fully not because of the disability itself, but precisely because of the failure of the environment to provide adequate experiences and special patterns of care. Thoughtful preparation of the classroom environment, as indicated by NAEYC (1986), Weikart (1979), and Morrison (1984), becomes increasingly important as classroom populations become more diverse.

Many teachers feel worried about mainstreaming children with specific educational needs into their classrooms because of their own lack of training in special education, and because of their fear of not knowing how to handle children who do not have the readiness skills to bring to the task of learning.

In recognizing the need to teach children, not curricula, the caring teacher will begin to think in terms of the characteristics of each individual learner. Some questions the teacher will want to ask are:

1. What am I trying to teach a child?

2. What skills are required to learn this task?

3. What does the particular child bring to the learning situation? (What must the child be able to do in order to learn the task, and which of the prerequisite skills does the child have?)

4. How should the material be organized and presented in order to meet the demands of the various learners?

5. How can each child become active in the learning process?

6. What can I learn from asking the child about that child's self-perceived difficulties? ("What do you need to learn to become a better reader?")

When teachers think less in terms of learning problems and more in terms of learning abilities, they naturally become more individualized in their educational program. There is an old social work adage of "starting where the client is." That is sound advice for teachers as well. Beginning with each student at that student's level of understanding ensures foundation building for further learning. Tuning into the individualized needs of students and meeting those needs are often less time consuming and less stressful for teachers than trying to maintain group control wherein everyone must behave and learn in the same way.

38 ■ STRATEGIES FOR TEACHING AND LEARNING

Mrs. Andrews knows that many of her first graders delight in their early afternoon quiet time. She plays soft music while the children relax, read books, or work on individual projects. Laneila, however, never seemed to enjoy this time, during which she became cranky and annoying. Laneila is a high-energy child who requires an unusual amount of stimulation and activity. Mrs. Andrews discovered that giving Laneila specific jobs to do during quiet time enabled her to expend her extra energy while utilizing this energy to benefit the classroom. Laneila was given the job of alphabetizing all of the books on the library shelves, washing the chalkboards daily, delivering messages to the office, picking up the afternoon snack, and emptying the wastebasket in the janitor's office, where she can talk and visit with the janitor. In this way, she contributes positively to the community, and her classmates appreciate her service efforts. At the end of the quiet time, Laneila, like the other children, is "rested" and is able to sit down for a 20-minute math period.

HOW CHILDREN LEARN

Chapters 2 and 3 developed the ideas of a learning process and the developmental differences that can affect how children learn. Contemporary research (Torgeson 1983; Short 1984; Meltzer 1990) proposes that an additional factor needs to be considered when looking at children's learning. The element of problem solving—strategies for approaching social and educational tasks—seems to play an important role in how successful children can function at home and at school. Researching the problem-solving approaches and metacognitive (thinking about thinking) strategies of learning disabled and non-learning disabled adolescents and adults has led these theorists to conclude that learning disabled students frequently use different processing routes and mental patterns. Their metacognitive processes operate differently, and they often display inefficient and inflexible strategies for problem solving and learning. Short (1990), Levine (1989), and Swanson (1989) concur with Meltzer (1990) and others that the problem-solving strategies of learning disabled students are markedly different from those of non-learning disabled students. Many learning disabled individuals appear to be "inefficient learners" (Swanson 1989) or "maladaptive learners" (Torgeson 1978).

These findings indicate that young children with learning differences may need to be taught not only the skills of specific subject matter, but also the strategies for approaching academic material. Students with various

How Children Learn ■ 39

learning differences manifest difficulties to which teachers will need to be attuned, particularly in the area of problem solving. Studies of problem-solving abilities and concept learning indicate that learning disabled students:

1. Have difficulty accessing, organizing, and coordinating incoming information.

2. Have trouble identifying critical attributes in tasks.

3. Are lacking in planning systematically.

4. Use feedback insufficiently.

5. Do not generalize from one situation to another.

Some children do not seem to solve everyday living "problems," let alone school-designated tasks. A kindergarten teacher suggests that there is a tendency on the part of adults to overlook the "obvious." She feels that the system often makes assumptions about a child's understanding of school vernacular: "Line up!" says the teacher. (What does that mean? How do you line up?) "Tell me," smiles the cafeteria cook. (Tell her what? What am I supposed to say?) "Clean those tables!" admonishes the art teacher. (How? With what?) A very bright math teacher remembers his third-grade experience with a teacher who consistently wrote on his spelling test papers (which were mostly wrong): "See me?" As a third grader, he had no idea what this meant as he could not see her on the paper, and did not know how to respond to her question. The teacher never followed up by "seeing him" either.

Teachers will need to help children figure out the basic survival skills, perhaps assigning a partner or buddy to support the less-capable child. Many children would feel more comfortable with a peer partner, which eliminates being singled out by the teacher. Although it is true that most children do learn appropriate school and social behaviors by a process of osmosis, some youngsters with variant learning styles do not internalize the environmental cues in a meaningful fashion. Skills which the other kids "just get," developmentally delayed youngsters need to have specifically taught. A frequent response to telling a young child about a "seemingly obvious" behavior is "Oh! I didn't know." If everyone in the room is standing up to say the Pledge of Allegiance, it would seem that one would "know" to stand. The child who remains seated may be viewed by the

40 ■ STRATEGIES FOR TEACHING AND LEARNING

teacher as being recalcitrant or oppositional, when in fact, the teacher never actually told the child to stand, and the child has not figured out what to do.

> Trevor transferred from a private to a public school in the third grade. He is an intellectually astute child who, it was assumed, "knew the rules." Several months after school began, the teacher complained to me that Trevor was always wandering around the classroom, reading books or looking at things when he finished his worksheets. That was permissible behavior in Trevor's former school but it was not acceptable in this classroom. I asked the teacher if she had ever told Trevor to sit down, or told him what to do when he finished his work. "No!" she snapped, "I thought a bright boy like that would know how to behave!"

Most teachers are able to figure out which children are absorbing information and which are not. If a child has been told the same thing numerous times and still is not doing it, or understanding it, the teacher might recognize that a new method of instruction needs to be introduced. This may be a good time to 1) watch the child at problem-solving tasks, and 2) ask the child some questions.

> An eight year old, Kathleen, reads sentences and short books much more competently than she reads sight words because she has learned to use context clues, pictures, and "surround" words to help her. In reading sight words for me, Kathleen read "open" as "once." I was having trouble figuring out how she arrived at "once," so I asked her about this. "Because the next word was 'upon'," she said blithely. "I guessed that the first word was once, like 'once upon a time.'" ("The book was open upon his lap.")

> Of course! Except that I never would have figured that out without hearing it from her. (Try to spell "once upon" phonetically: "whuns a pon.")

It is smart to talk with children about their own learning, and to share ideas back with them. Many of the most successful strategies come straight from students themselves. Furthermore, asking children about their problem-solving approaches enables the teacher to discern which methods the student uses that are efficient and those that are inefficient or cause confusion. Mistakes are not made randomly, but have patterns which the teacher will want to observe. Asking the child about problem-solving approaches also gives children an opportunity to think about their own thinking, a process which can be extremely useful.

Aaron tells me that he is "tired of sounding words out!" At school, Aaron has been taught to read phonetically for three years, but he still reads at a low first-grade level. I ask him what he thinks would work better for him, and he immediately responds: "Memorizing them." Aaron has memorized more baseball statistics than any child his age I have ever met, so I suppose he may be right about being able to memorize reading words also. We start with word families, not by sounds, but by sight, and we write a story about Cat and the Fat Bat. Aaron loves it! The next week, he wants to write about Gall, the Small Ball. The tasks get harder months later as we have run out of rhyming words but by this time, Aaron is beginning to think of himself as a "reader" after all, and he is more willing to tackle blends, phonemes, prefixes, and suffixes.

Danielle is a seven-year-old gymnastics enthusiast. Every day after school, she spends hours at the gym, where she successfully remembers rather long and complicated routines. Her teacher and parents puzzle over this because memory deficits seem to be the cause of her school problems. Danielle has trouble holding onto information which is presented either visually or auditorily, but no one at school has taken advantage of her kinesthetic memory. When I ask Danielle how she remembers her gymnastics routines, she answers unequivocally, "I feel them in my body." Danielle will benefit in school work by being given many manipulatives with which to work out problems. She needs to get out of her seat and walk in front of the desk to remember what "in front of" feels like. She needs to make associations between words/concepts with which her body is already familiar: *on top of* (walking on top of the balance beam), *more* (more practice), *before* (before the judge lowers the flag).

Rather than being overwhelmed by a classroom full of many children with varying learning styles, teachers can take heart in this phenomenon because on any given day or with any given approach, the teacher is likely to reach at least some of the children. Another day, if the teacher wants to try something new, the odds are that he or she will reach a few children or more that time also. This makes teaching and learning more engaging and challenging, and there is less opportunity for either the teacher or the students to feel bored.

BEHAVIOR MANAGEMENT

The adjustment of children to school is influenced by their temperament, psychosocial maturity, and general developmental progress as much as it is by the classroom environment and the personality of the teacher. It is the interaction of all of these components which will determine how a child adapts to "a place called school" (Goodlad 1984). It is understood that attentive teachers will make instructional adjustments to particular students' cognitive needs; but it is not always true that affective behaviors are attended to with that same sensitivity and individualization. Although not all young children with learning difficulties display psychosocial troubles, many of them do; most notably as they get older, and especially if their academic deficits have not been addressed.

Research (Swanson and Keogh 1990; Kronick 1988) indicates that many learning disabled children differ from their peers in areas outside of the classroom, usually in their social interactions. It is difficult to have significant educational deficits without having some emotional overlay or social dysfunction also. Wagner and Kistner (1990) write that "The frequency with which learning disabled children experience failure would seem to tax their abilities to maintain adaptive beliefs about themselves" (p. 84). Sometimes extraordinarily bright children display cognitive-affective discrepancies (Comfort 1988; MacCoby 1983; Roedell 1984) which result in behavioral difficulties; and students with specific physical handicaps or cultural differences probably will manifest behaviors which require particular attention from their teachers as well. Teachers will want to incorporate interactional learning strategies into their teaching plans so that the affective domain of education can be enhanced along with the cognitive domain.

Children with learning and living difficulties show a variety of behavioral styles. As discussed earlier, many are poor readers of social cues and are relatively oblivious to behavioral postures and to nonverbal communications of their peers. Some appear to be inattentive and disorganized (often as a result of a clinical attention deficit or because of memory dysfunctions), while others seem to be rigid and stubborn (because they over-focus on small details or because deviation from routine confuses and disorients them). Since many children with learning difficulties have proven to be poor problem solvers, it is probable that they are also deficient in their abilities to improvise, generalize, or initiate problem-solving approaches in their social relationships or in their classroom behaviors. Youngsters who have trouble with academic and practical intelligence tend not to be very malleable or adaptive, which makes them difficult to be with as playmates. An example of this is the exceptionally bright, moralistic child who knows the literal rules of the game, but who cannot adjust to the give-and-take mores of how peers play the game.

Kronick (1988) accurately (and amusingly) points out that children with learning difficulties are inefficient in amalgamating peer-appropriate behaviors, at which time teachers and parents make "one of our biggest errors in the teaching of social skills: We inculcate teacher-pleasing behaviors because peer appropriate behavior often displeases adults considerably!" (p. 98).

In assessing how to manage a child's behavior, it is useful to observe what the child does in a given situation. All children do not behave in the same way for the same reasons at the same time. Penicillin works beautifully against strep throat unless the patient is allergic to penicillin. Similarly, each student must be helped to gain control over his or her own behavior in a way which has relevant meaning to that child individually. There is not a generic recipe. A teacher's stern look may have monumental effects on one child, and no influence whatsoever on another. Certainly, the highly active and distractible child requires a different behavior management program from the withdrawn or passive child. Some children behave poorly in a classroom because they have low thresholds for noise or for visual stimulation. Extremely intense students or those who have idiosyncratic sensitivities may not do well in normal, active classroom environments.

Teachers who do not understand the variations of behavioral styles, who require highly disciplined classrooms, or who run very loosely organized rooms are likely to be providing environments which are problematic for the less adaptive student. Power struggles or underachievement are common outcomes of these situations.

Teachers will do well to remember that in academic problems, the information needed to solve a problem is more obvious than it is in practical or social problems. In social interaction, it is often necessary to glean what is important from seemingly unrelated information. If Jackie does not want to play four-square, it may be because she is not feeling well, she doesn't like the group of children who are playing, her mother told her not to get her dress dirty, or because she is in a bad mood since she forgot her homework in the car. There are varying reasons for Jackie's not wanting to play, and varying solutions as to how her not playing four-square might be resolved. Many children with learning difficulties, however, are just not very proficient in these deciphering skills, so they have trouble figuring out what is important in group interaction. It also is not very apparent to children with social perception deficits when it is advantageous to conform, and when it may be more beneficial not to do so. Many youngsters with learning difficulties get set up by peers to get into trouble because others recognize that the unconventional child has poor social judgment.

On the other hand, it is also true that some children with quite specific learning deficits are wonderful socially, or athletically, and only suffer during the class time during which their disability is tapped. Young children in particular are not at all critical of a child who has trouble in math and spelling if the child can keep up socially and playfully. Boys tend to value athletic prowess over academic ability. Adults warm up to youngsters who are sweet and polite even though the child has reading difficulties. It is the child who behaves negatively and interacts poorly who will require additional teacher and parent intervention.

From behavioral psychology and the field of applied behavioral analysis comes the term *behavior modification*. Strictly speaking, behavior modification is a systematic approach to altering behavior through reinforcement, and the arranging of environmental events so that a specific change in observable behavior results. Not so strictly speaking, behavior tends to be modified throughout one's life as an individual seeks to maintain meaningful balance in the many-changing environments of everyday living. Teachers of young children will benefit themselves and their students if they can teach with both flexibility and purpose, adapting their own behavior to meet individual needs at the same time as they teach and request modification of children's behaviors.

ACCOMMODATING FOR DIFFERENCES

The process of integrating young children with developmental delays into the regular classroom can sometimes be less difficult than it may originally seem because all good developmentally appropriate early childhood programs emphasize active learning and discovery, which is exactly what the delayed child needs. Teachers need to be familiar with the ages and stages of early childhood development. Teachers of young children will want to expect and tolerate substantial differences in children's engagement in various activities, verbal communication, and readiness for "seat work." Literacy behaviors, as experienced through representational play, storytelling, and involvement with words and numbers, will vary enormously according to a child's strengths, weaknesses, and interests. Standard early education practices which are developmentally oriented are appropriate for all children, whether or not they have special needs.

Specific instructional accommodations may include teaching to a particular strength, such as using many visual cues for the child who is very strong visually and weaker auditorily; or attending to a specific weakness, such as providing a partner to help the child who has trouble following verbal directions. Children who process material slowly may do best by being given small amounts of information at a time. Breaking a task into small pieces is effective for most young children. Teacher tolerance for those who need to ask many questions or who need to have material repeated frequently is hard to maintain, but it is important that one do so as much as possible. Patience is helpful for these children in that it reduces their anxiety. For those children who do not acquire information incidentally, certain behaviors and expectations need to be modeled and explained.

All of these "adjustments" pertain less to content than to method of instruction. When a teacher reads a story, it will never mean the exact same thing to each and every listener. Each child will visualize, fantasize, assimilate, and extend the plot, characters, and setting within his or her own frame of reference and experience. Similarly, when a game is played, children will enjoy the game in a variety of ways. One child may want more turns, another more chips, and another more points. One child will count each of the four dots on the die while another will recognize the configuration as four. Each of us takes in what we can and how we can according to what we already know and according to how adaptable we are to accommodating new ideas and information. The facilitating teacher will encourage children at all ability levels to expand upon ideas, concepts, strategies, and possibilities, and to think about the ideas promulgated by the child's peers. In real life, there are very few right and wrong answers. Successful adults are not necessarily those who are exceptionally intelligent intellectually, but those who are skillful at incorporating, utilizing, and enriching the ideas of their cohorts.

In 1981, Reid and Hresko suggested that learning disabled students do not seem to learn in a way which is fundamentally different from non-learning disabled students, but "their learning is less efficient and apparently developmentally delayed" (p. 51). Their research results showed that learning disabled students often had the abilities needed for a task but that they failed to use them spontaneously in the appropriate situations. When specifically instructed to use certain skills, however, they did so. Reid and Hresko concluded that the acquisition of a skill is not enough. (Not whether a child *can* do something, but whether the child *does* do it.) In other words, a child must not only have access to the use of the skill, but the child must also know when to call upon that skill. This requires coordination of a number of ability processes simultaneously. Both school and life make fairly heavy demands on coordinated processing; yet, information-processing components tend to be the weak features of many students with learning disabilities (Swanson 1988). Short and Feagans (1990) also found that problem-solving skills are deficient in many students with learning difficulties.

Problem solving is a part of everyone's life, regardless of socioeconomic or academic levels. Meltzer, Solomon, and Fenton (1987) found that the steps in the problem-solving process have proven to be problematic for those learners who seem to be less efficient than their non-learning disabled counterparts vis-à-vis planning, self-monitoring, and approaching problems. They are less flexible in the selection of strategies, and they have trouble moving from one aspect of the problem to another. Although Torgesen (1982) referred to such students as "inactive learners," Swanson (1988) contended that they were often very active, but that their activity was inefficient.

Active learning has become the vanguard word of the last decade, with parents and teachers being charged with the responsibility of structuring materials and environments which provide for and promote maximum learning. Essentially, active learning involves metacognitive strategies, meaning that both the student and the teacher, or the child and the parent, are posing problem-solving and awareness questions. Thinking aloud facilitates the process and allows for the development and sharing of ideas. The teacher might want to model the approach to a problem-solving situation by presenting a task and by asking the following questions:

- What has to be learned/produced?

- What do I already know about this topic?

- How shall I organize myself and the material to get started?

- How will I know when I know the information?

- What should I do to be sure that I don't forget it?

The basic strategies involved in an active learning paradigm involve thinking aloud (asking questions) and discovering. From the teacher's perspective, the learning process becomes less declaration and more discovery. Rather than telling Peter that one cup of water is twice as much as a half cup of water, the teacher might ask Peter to bring several cups, jars, funnels, and bowls of water to the table for the children to have them available. The teacher might question if there is anything the same or different about the amounts of water which various jars hold; or the teacher may ask if there is a relationship between the green cup (a 1/2-cup) and the red cup (a whole cup) in terms of how much water each holds.

Frank Smith equates discovery learning to bike riding in that you "got to up and do it!" None of the talking about how to ride a bike will be quite the same as the actual riding. Discovery learning is often misunderstood or misrepresented. Some people assume that children will spontaneously discover all that life has to offer. In fact, discovery learning is most effective when the teacher has done a considerable amount of pre-planning and setting of the stage. Classroom activities always need to be constructed with cognitive and developmental levels in mind, and materials must be age and task specific. The opportunity to discover needs to be made available.

Nevertheless, even when all of this is in place, most researchers in the field of learning disabilities concur that many students with specific learning differences still "don't get it," or it may take them five or six times as many trials as their peers before they do get it. They may need to reconstruct the situations over and over, repeating an experience far more frequently before they internalize it than do their classmates. Moreover, the developmentally delayed child may not be able to transfer the lesson learned from one situation to another, so that each experience feels like an entirely new one.

> A seventh grader was taught how to read daily temperatures on a graph. It took him quite a long time to learn to do this, and he was often confused. Ultimately, he seemed to have grasped the process, but when he was asked to graph monthly rainfall levels on another graph, the child was totally baffled and saw no connection between these two tasks.

Students with particular reading difficulties may sound out the same word each and every time it is encountered. The word does not become integrated, memorized, or learned; it is always a new word to be tackled. Similarly, a child may not comprehend that 4 + 7 is the same as 7 + 4 if the meaning of this addition fact has not been fully understood. Each of these problems will be seen as a different one—even as late as the sixth or seventh grade for the learning-delayed child—and one will observe this child counting on fingers or using touch math to count seven more than four and four more than seven.

In summary, children with learning variations tend to have inefficient problem-solving strategies, and they tend to underuse skills which they do have. They have difficulty with linking, or generalizing, appropriate skills and strategies from one situation to another. The latter often manifests itself in one of two ways: either the child has a strategy which worked once, so the child uses it over and over everywhere whether it applies or not; or, the child has learned a good strategy for memorizing events in history class, but does not recognize that the same strategy could be employed for learning authors in literature class. As teaching adults, we must make the connections for these children and help them to see recurrent patterns.

A cognitive approach to remediating these difficulties encourages the student to become active in the learning process. Special-needs students, from the time they are very young, will have to be taught meaningful steps for learning. They must be directed to build on their knowledge base, ask themselves questions, rehearse the material, and devise plans for studying and monitoring their work. The stories, songs, and rhymes which are so much a part of good preschool classes are wonderfully conducive to active learning. Participation, involvement, and high-interest-level material have proven to be effective in augmenting cognitive awareness and learning success, but too often these aspects of education wane beyond the early years of school. More than other students, the child with learning difficulties is especially dependent upon participatory learning in order to enhance and make meaningful the educational experience.

Throughout this book I have stressed that I do not believe that there are specific teaching/learning strategies which come with guarantees. Nevertheless, certain learning dysfunctions generally do respond to particular treatment modalities or to particular teaching techniques. No matter what else one does, it is best to be predictable, consistent, and structured. Beyond that, many teachers find it useful to keep a good observation record of each child's behavior, strengths, weaknesses, interests, abilities, and so forth. A teacher may want to make a chart which will help to map out and clarify certain patterns. The teacher should ask:

- What is the dysfunction?
- How is it manifested?
- What effect is it having? (cognitive, academic, behavioral)
- What intervention may be useful?

Table 4.1 describes broad-based, umbrella-like learning dysfunctions. This should be viewed only as a guideline because no student is going to fall into these categories absolutely. For a more detailed description of learning problems and prescriptions for classroom accommodations, see Lynn Meltzer and Bethany Solomon, *Educational Prescriptions for the Classroom*, 1988; and for a chart depicting low-severity learning disabilities and their outcomes, see Melvin Levine, *Common Development Dysfunctions in School Children*. Both of these are available through Educators Publishing Service, Inc., 75 Moulton Street, Cambridge, MA 02238-9101.

Table 4.1

Broad-based Learning Deficits

Dysfunction	Manifestation	Effects	Accommodations
Attention problems	Temperamental irregularities Overactivity Impulsivity Cognitive fatigue	Poor planning and monitoring Erratic/careless Inconsistent Trouble with directions	Regular classroom routine Awareness of teacher expectations Short work periods Organizational aids Discussion of schedule changes Private time with teacher each day
Visual-spatial	Accident proneness Directional confusion Motor difficulty Letter reversal Delayed reading/writing readiness	Figure-ground confusion Poor word attack/decode ability Poor spelling Awkward writing Digit/letter reversals Listening skills better than reading comprehension skills	Activities which emphasize directionality and spatial awareness Tracking exercises Matching tasks Tactile aids Whole language or phonics-based reading program Graph paper for math
Temporal-sequential	Delayed concept of time Seriation difficulty Trouble following instructions Logical sequence difficulties Letter/digit order confusion Slow in copying Poor spelling	Poor sequential memory Trouble with multi-step processing Seems inattentive Impaired verbal reasoning Spelling/number disorganization Can't follow directions	Use clocks, calendars, day-timers, repetitions Write out task steps Object seriation Mnemonic devices Context clues Color coding Automatization of basic information Visual presentation of material

(Table 4.1 continues on page 50.)

50 ■ STRATEGIES FOR TEACHING AND LEARNING

Table 4.1 (*continued*)

Dysfunction	Manifestation	Effects	Accommodations
Language difficulties	Speech or language acquisition delay Articulation problems Not able to be understood Can't find right word Difficulty retelling a story Limited verbal expression Frequently says "What?" May be shy or withdrawn	Poor language understanding Diminished vocab. Reading/writing/spelling difficulties Math word-problem difficulties Limited class participation Social withdrawal	Preferential seating Repetition Use of tapes and computers Written directions Read to self, not aloud Whole-word reading Language experience methods Franklin Speller Reading comprehension skills

GOOD STRATEGIES FOR ALL TEACHERS

- Understand early childhood development.

- Be consistent and predictable.

- Be sensitive to temperamental and learning style differences.

- Ask identifiable questions:
    - What am I trying to teach?
    - What are several different means of teaching this task?
    - What expectations do I have of the child who needs to learn this task?

- Look at a child's method of problem solving.
    - Is it a good method? Will it work in this situation?
    - How can I help the child to strategize more effectively?

- Observe behavior. What is the behavior saying about the student's feelings and about the style of coping?

- Devise an individualized behavior program which is specific to the needs and the abilities of the particular child.

- Allow for and utilize differences. Recognize that all students won't learn the same thing in a given lesson.

- Model problem-solving processes. Show various ways of approaching a problem. Ask for student input.

REFERENCE LIST

Comfort, Randy Lee. (1985) *The Child Care Catalog*. Littleton, CO: Libraries Unlimited.

_____. (1988) Cognitive-Affective Discrepancies in Three Gifted Boys. Ph.D. diss., University of Denver, CO.

Cruickshank, W., F. Bentzen, F. Ratzeburg, and M. Tannhauser. (1961) *A Teaching Method for Brain-Injured and Hyperactive Children*. Syracuse, NY: Syracuse University Press.

Feagans, L., B. Short, and L. Meltzer, eds. (1990) *Learning Disability Subtypes*. Hillsdale, NJ: Erlbaum.

Goodlad, John. (1984) *A Place Called School: Prospects for the Future*. New York: McGraw-Hill.

Greenspan, Stanley. (1988) Fostering emotional and social development in infants with disabilities. *Zero to Three* 9, no. 1.

Hohmann, Gary, Bernard Banet, and David Weikart. (1979) *Young Children in Action*. Ypsilanti, MI: High/Scope Press.

Katz, L. G., J. D. Raths, and R. D. Torres. (1987) *A Place Called Kindergarten*. Urbana, IL: Clearing House in Elementary & Early Childhood Education, p. 29.

Kronick, Doreen. (1988). *New Approaches to Learning Disabilities*. Philadelphia: Greene and Stratton.

Levine, M. (1983) *Common Developmental Dysfunctions in School Children*. Cambridge, MA: Educators Publishing Service.

MacCoby, Eleanor E., Norman Garmezy, and Michael Rutter, eds. (1983) Social Emotional Development and Response to Stressors. *Stress, Coping, and Development in Children*. New York: McGraw-Hill, p. 217-33.

Meltzer, Lynn, Ph.D. (1990) Problem-Solving Strategies and Academic Performance in Learning Disabled Students: Do Subtypes Exist? *Learning Disability Subtypes*. Edited by L. Feagans, B. Short, and L. Meltzer. Hillsdale, NJ: Erlbaum.

Meltzer, Lynn, Ph.D., and Bethany Solomon, M.A. (1988) *Educational Prescriptions for the Classroom for Students with Learning Problems*. Cambridge, MA: Educators Publishing.

Meltzer, L. J., B. Solomon, and T. Fenton. (1987) Problem-solving strategies in children with and without learning disabilities. Paper presented at the 95th Annual Convention of the American Psychological Association, New York.

Mitchell, Anne, Michelle Seligson, and Fern Marx. (1989) *Early Childhood Programs and the Public Schools*. Boston: Auburn House.

Morrison, George. (1984) *Early Childhood Education Today*. Columbus, OH: Charles E. Merrill Publishing.

National Association for the Education of Young Children. (1986) *Good Teaching Practices for 4- and 5-year Olds*. NAEYC Position Paper, Washington, DC.

Reid, Kim, and Wayne Hresko. (1981) *A Cognitive Approach to Learning Disabilities*. New York: McGraw-Hill.

Roedell, Wendy C. (1984) Vulnerabilities of highly gifted children. *Roeper Review* 6, no. 3: 127-30.

Short, E. J., C. L. Cuddy, S. E. Friebert, and C. Schatschneider. (1990) The diagnostic and educational utility of thinking aloud during problem solving. In: *Learning Disabilities: Theoretical Research Issues*. Edited by L. Swanson and B. Keogh. Hillsdale, NJ: Lawrence Erlbaum Associates.

Short, E. J., and E. B. Ryan. (1984) Metacognitive differences between skilled and less skilled readers: Remediating deficits through story grammar and attribution training. *Journal of Educational Psychology* 76: 225-35.

Swanson, H. L. (1988) Learning disabled children's problem solving: Identifying mental processes underlying intelligent performance. *Intelligence* 12, no. 3: 261-78.

———. (1989) Strategy instruction: Overview of principles and procedures for effective use. *Learning Disability Quarterly* 12, no. 1: 3-14.

Swanson, Lee, and Barbara Keogh. (1990) *Learning Disabilities: Theoretical Research Issues*. Hillsdale, NJ: Lawrence Erlbaum Associates.

Torgesen, J. K. (1978) Performance of reading disabled children on serial memory tasks: A selective review of recent research. *Reading Research Quarterly* 14: 57-87.

———. (1982) The learning disabled child as an inactive learner: Educational implications. *Topics in Learning and Learning Disabilities* 2, no. 1: 45-51.

Torgesen, J. K., and B. Licht. (1983) The learning-disabled child as an inactive learner: Retrospects and prospects. In: *Current Topics in Learning Difficulties* 1: 3-31. Edited by J. McKinney and L. Feagans. Norwood, NJ: Ablex.

Wagner, Richard, and Janet Kistner. (1990) Implications of the distinction between academic and practical intelligence for learning disabled children. In: *Learning Disabilities*. Edited by L. Swanson and B. Keogh. Hillsdale, NJ: Lawrence Erlbaum Associates.

5

Teaching and Learning to Read and Write

It's hard not remembering. Sometimes I even forget what I'm going to write.
—Fifth-grade girl

It's hard not knowing the vocabulary enough to understand it.
—Sixth-grade girl

Sometimes I space to outer space and I miss parts of learning. I need to read things out loud to understand them.
—Fourth-grade boy

It's strange about Tory. The other third-grade teachers and I find ourselves talking about him frequently. He comes from a home where the parents read to their children all of the time, and he certainly seems to be a smart little boy. Many complex concepts make sense to Tory. He knows quite a bit about a lot of different kinds of things. His speech and his listening comprehension are very mature. Nevertheless, he can't read. He can hardly read more than his name and maybe a half dozen words. It's such a puzzle to me! Why can't Tory seem to get the letters and words together?
—Third-grade teacher

> *It makes me angry that I can't read. I feel really stupid even though my parents keep saying I'm not. Sometimes when I can't read the words I know I should know, I get really mad and my head erupts.*
> —Tory, 9 years old

LANGUAGE COMMUNICATION

The acquisition of language, both for understanding and for communicating, is essential for meaningful interactions in a developed society. Although various theorists have classified language learning in different ways, it is generally agreed that there are three main components which contribute to verbal communication.

1. Inner language (Vygotsky 1962)/Preoperational thought (Piaget 1962)—what goes on inside one's head; what we say to ourselves.

2. Receptive language—what is taken in, understood, and processed.

3. Expressive language—what is said or written.

Virtually all theorists also contend that the purpose of language is interactional (Bloom and Lahey 1978). A person needs words to express thoughts in order to tell about something. As was discussed in the previous chapter, this is a knowledge-based developmental process, meaning that a child will initially use what the child already knows. Before understanding about subcategories of liquids, for instance, a toddler may ask for more milk, when the child really wants more juice, but the toddler does not know the word "juice," so the child says, "More milk." Preschoolers often refer to their instructor as "teacher" or "mommy" before they have associated the teacher with a name, while "He's a daddy" may actually mean "He's an adult male."

Listening to a child's developmental level of language can be a very good indicator of the student's readiness for reading and writing. The previous examples, for instance, are appropriate for two- to three-year-olds, but not for five- and six-year-olds. The first grader who still communicates in this fashion needs to develop a much broader and stronger language foundation before the child will be ready to read or to write.

While there are many unanswered questions in the area of language acquisition, it seems that a connection between cognition and language often exists. Language is dependent upon an appreciation of words as symbols and upon an understanding of the sequencing of words which convey meaning. The young child must recognize that the word "book" is a symbolic representation of the actual book. The child who wants to ask permission to go to the bathroom must understand which words to use in which order to accomplish the task. "Desk pencil bathroom play" will not convey the same message as "I need to go to the bathroom." Children with language dysfunctions have trouble assimilating and generalizing the rules of language.

On the other hand, there are cognitively bright children who have language deficits or speech defects. The hearing impaired and those with cerebral palsy are notable examples. Although it is not unusual for a variety of speech and language delays to occur in children who are average or above average intellectually, it would be unique for a cognitively limited student to use an advanced vocabulary and well-developed language communication skills.

It is typically assumed that various birth defects, sensory or environmental deprivations, experiential limitations, or emotional disturbances can contribute to language delays. Neurological disorders may or may not affect language development also. Some children do not begin to talk within the average age range; others do speak, but with language dysfunctions. Even though the classroom teacher is not expected to diagnose the cause or particular anomalies of a speech disorder, the teacher, like the parent, is in a good position to identify a language delay. Teachers who have experience with many young children will know which children are speaking in patterns, sequences, styles, or tones which differentiate them from their playmates.

In the doll house or dress-up corner, there may be one child who is always designated as "the baby." *Sometimes* this is because the "baby" child does not speak as well as the other children. Some children never or rarely volunteer verbal information. They may "show," but they do not "tell." Youngsters with certain auditory processing problems ask a zillion questions, "What did you say?" being par for the course. The child who "affects" baby talk is actually much more advanced in language skills than the child who can really only speak in "Me want it" terms. The first student may be experiencing emotional or behavioral dysfunctions, while the second child may be manifesting oral communication deficits.

Especially in the early years, it is very hard to separate cognition from language development. They are enormously interrelated and interdependent. A preschool or kindergarten teacher will want to figure out if the child is capable of representational thinking. Does the child understand a symbolic meaning or function of a concept? Uzgiris and Hunt (1975) have developed play assessments for very young children which enable the evaluator to observe a child's ability to substitute symbolic material for "the real thing." Can a child pretend to eat with a stick, for instance, rather than a spoon? Can a child push a box, calling it a car, stroller, or fire engine? The young student's capacity to enter into symbolic play with objects, imagery, drawing, and role playing will be indicative of that child's cognitive development. If oral communication is not relatively commensurate with (if it lags behind) non-linguistic representational play, one might consider the possibility of a language delay.

Non-linguistic communication also is an important part of language development. As was discussed in the section on social and affective development, many children with learning difficulties stumble over learning to read body postures, facial expressions, and physical proximities. Expressively, they may be weak transmitters of their own nonverbal messages; and at the same time, receptively, they are poor translators of the incoming cues.

Most children with speech and language dysfunctions need more professional remediation than can be devised by the regular classroom teacher, but the teacher has a very major role to play in terms of augmenting the speech therapist's recommendations and in providing both individual and group opportunities in which the child can practice developing skills. On the other hand, some children who do not have significant speech deficits may present minor language delays which can be remediated quite nicely. The teacher will need to facilitate multisensory paths of communication.

There are children whose language is delayed because older siblings speak for them, because they live in bilingual families, because they have little environmental experience with being spoken to, read to, or listened to. These children will thrive in classrooms which are rich in opportunities to listen to records, tapes, and stories, and to interact with more language-experienced children and adults. Songs and dramatic play are important for all young children, but especially so for those whose language development is slow.

The preschool and kindergarten teacher will want to verbalize for the child many of the child's actions. "I see you are building a tower. You have a red block at the top of the tower," and the teacher will, in turn, request that children talk about their own play, "Can you tell me what is happening in your picture? Who are these people in the doll house? What are they doing?" Mutual storytelling is very effective, as is partnering, where two or three children work on a project together. While a child may not be ready to answer a teacher's direct question of "Tell me about your picture," the child may be found talking with a peer about a T.V. show or about a story read in class.

There are many worthwhile books which aid the preschool/kindergarten teacher in selecting appropriate language-oriented and pre-reading/writing activities (see appendix B). As always, a multisensory language experience approach will be effective with the most number of children. Songs and poems that rhyme are particularly helpful for tuning children into the phonetic sounds of blends and vowels. Stencil drawings and finger or pencil tracings encourage children to think about directionality of writing. Putting story pictures in order facilitates sequential organization and relationships of parts to wholes. Writing one's own name and the names of friends is more meaningful than copying words out of a workbook. Signing-in in the morning is a good way of practicing to write one's name, and also to learn from other children about how to make letters or write their names. "I have a D in my name; I'll show you how to make it." "I know how to spell your name. Can you spell mine too?" Children should be helped to write words which they ask about, and words which are of interest to them personally, so that writing begins to have purpose and meaning. Labeling pictures is another good technique for learning how to write everyday words.

> Maya learned to read and write very early, not because she was taught to do so, but because she "needed" words. "I have to send my doll a letter," she told her mother. "How do you spell 'cat'? Now how do you write 'hide'?"

> Similarly, Simon "needed" to read because he loved horses and wanted to know more about them. Picture books were not informative enough for this five-year-old. He repeatedly asked, "What do the pictures say?"

Children with speech and language deficits may be those the teacher finds more often involved in physical activities, in the art corner, at the building table, or in individual play, as opposed to those children who are engaged in activities which are interactive, such as drama, pretend, dress up, storytelling, singing, and board games. While solitary play need not be discouraged, language and social interaction should be brought in as often as possible.

It is relatively predictable that the first- or second-grade child who experiences major language deficits will have trouble with learning to read and to write. While there are many possible reasons for reading difficulties, language facility seems to be closely linked to the acquisition of reading and writing skills. Furthermore, unattended "mild" language delays often do not go the route of *Leo the Late Bloomer* (by Robert Kraus) who grew out of his immaturities—they linger on, with increasing impact as the child moves through school. Many of these dysfunctions emerge more remarkably or become more problematic in the fourth, fifth, and sixth grades as the demand for reading and writing becomes greater. A very typical example is the student who experiences phonetic weaknesses which interfere with spelling. One observes a child with a wonderfully rich oral vocabulary, who epitomizes the "minimalist" form when asked to write reports, essays, compositions, or journals. The child will employ only those basic words which the child has memorized for spelling tests because it is too hard to try to figure out the proper spelling of other words, or to correct so many mistakes.

Sometimes parents are surprised to hear that their middle-school-age child has "developed" language arts difficulties. More than likely, the child always experienced soft-sign weaknesses which did not emerge problematically until they were more specifically stressed. Reading, for example, in first and second grades focuses mostly on word recognition and on decoding skills. In the subsequent years, however, reading comprehension is emphasized. Similarly, very little writing is expected in the early years, while a substantial number of reports and essays are required in middle school.

Reading is a "many splendored thing," which brings knowledge, joy, relaxation, humor, and love into the lives of those who appreciate reading as vocation or avocation. Judging by the rising illiteracy rate, however, and listening to the multitude of students who experience reading/writing difficulties, one might surmise that many Americans are deprived of the opportunity to learn and to live through the written word. In Western cultures, one's knowledge base begins to suffer if one is not a reader, and one's vocational choices become severely limited in a society which is highly dependent upon literacy skills.

Chall (1983) emphasized the link between reading readiness stages and early childhood development, advising that a child's ability to integrate reading and writing into the child's educational experience is linked to the child's ability to incorporate and appreciate the child's personal environment. The development of reading, like the development of child growth, says Chall, presupposes a series of stages in which skills built in one level are carried into and utilized in the subsequent level. Brown and Palincsar (1984) support this viewpoint, suggesting that the reading schema most likely to succeed is that which utilizes the reader's knowledge base by matching and stretching the learner's life experience.

There is an enormous variety of programs available for teaching reading, some more popular or widely used than others. The Orton Society has found a phonetic approach (particularly the Slingerland method) to be a useful one for helping dyslexics to improve their reading skills. Some schools rely on basal readers, but many more utilize process teaching programs which include Readers' and Writers' Workshop techniques. Each program appears to have some validity for some students, but none is the absolute answer for every student. This is probably true because of the fact that students have individual styles of acquiring information, and a method that is effective for one student may not work with another.

Researchers all acknowledge that one's language experiences prior to school entry will play into a student's reading/writing acquisition ability. As was previously discussed, children with receptive or expressive language delays may have more trouble learning to read and to write than most of their peers do. Children with limited environmental experiences are likely to be slower in developing reading comprehension skills than those who have had broader exposure to the world around them. A story about a child being lost at the zoo will elicit empathy and understanding from the child who knows what a zoo is and/or the child who has been lost. Another child lacking this knowledge or experience may be slower to relate to the story. In some cases, it is critical to have particular background knowledge in order to have a story make sense, even if one can read and understand all of the words printed. A fascinating and poignant example of the importance and influence of a reader's knowledge is illustrated in the following passage, excerpted from Bransford and Johnson (1972).

> A newspaper is better than a magazine, and on a seashore is a better place than a street. At first it is better to run than to walk.... Birds seldom get too close.... If there are no complications, it can be very peaceful. A rock will serve as an anchor....

It is likely that the reader of this book was able to read and understand each word in the above passage; yet, it is probable that the reader did not understand the passage and could not explain what it is about. By supplying a knowledge base and informing the reader that the paragraph is about kites, a whole new dimension of comprehension will be added.

The implication is that a reader usually benefits substantially when prior knowledge can be brought to the text's contents. Children with learning difficulties may be limited in their amount of background knowledge.

One practical teacher suggests that whatever approach has been tried with a child and which has not acquired positive results should be discarded because the child associates it with failure. If the student is not learning to sound out words, to decode them phonetically, then any association between phonics and reading will be a set-up for defeat. The teacher must explore an entirely new system with this non-reader.

Language Communication ■ 61

Although examples of various reading strategies will be outlined subsequently, one always must be attentive to the strengths and weaknesses of the individual student without trying to find generic recipes. A broad, eclectic, open mind will serve the teacher well. Student involvement also becomes a critical element in the process. Currently, teachers talk about "interviewing" the child. The vernacular of interviewing is much too formal for me, but it has the same result as my "talking with a child." Ask the child frequently how the child arrived at the words read; why the child thought the sentence meant what the child understood it to mean; how the child remembered what was in the passage just read. Much of what we learn about students comes from the students themselves. Below are two examples of how or why children "invent" the spelling they do.

> A third-grade child in New York writes, "I live near Sentrul Borc," which is phonetically correct with a New York accent, but a little hard to understand if one teaches in Nebraska.

> Phonetically, it is also correct to write: "Fone Fred in Foenix to send fotografs from Filadelfia." (A student must be taught to memorize which words begin with "ph" rather than with "f".)

There are many anomalies in the English language which make it a difficult language to read and to spell, but some students seem to learn about the idiosyncrasies and about the regularities more easily than others. Children with specific language and auditory deficits tend to have more difficulties than others. It is often not appropriate to dwell on phonics with this group, precisely because of the homonyms and irregularities of the sounds of the English language:

ate/eight	funny/money	read/read/red
p<u>n</u>eumonia		
k<u>n</u>ob	stuff rhymes with tough	
g<u>n</u>u	t<u>ough</u> does not rhyme with d<u>ough</u>	

A cognitively bright fourth-grade child says, "I just wanted to award you of the situation." This is not a youngster with language deficits. He has made a verb tense error, but the meaning is logical and clear. A fifth grader, however, is concerned about the amount of time the assessment testing is going to take. He asks: "How long does this building take?" His actual concern is "Will I be finished with testing in time to go to soccer?" Expressive language, word retrieval, and sequencing are problematic areas for this student.

An emerging kindergarten writer with very good language skills writes of going to see a "museem zibit." A less well-developed, but equally enthusiastic writer has put a large "B - E" on her page. When asked what her story says, she reads: "B, E spells 'Sit on your bottom!'" In the third grade, one might have cause for concern. In kindergarten, both of these stories portray a good understanding of words, meanings, and symbolic representation connecting thoughts, words, and the writing of them.

Some children do better when they visualize and memorize the sight of a word. In fact, good readers never sound out every word because they have, indeed, learned to recognize many hundreds of words. Only when an unfamiliar word is encountered will the reader need to apply a decoding strategy. An equally good strategy may be to skip the word or to substitute another word for it. It is useful to teach young children who are weak in the phonetic area to memorize the 100 most commonly used words in the English language (Fitzgerald 1951). Children who have spelling difficulties will benefit from memorizing and making automatic the recognition and correct spelling of this list. As these students progress through school, it is expedient to help them to identify the consistent prefixes and suffixes, and to automatize various spelling rules, such as "i before e except after c." Breaking the word into visual pieces rather than into phonetic syllables is often helpful for the visual learner:

talk (ing)   talk (s)   talk (ed)

Word families can be utilized successfully, if differently, with auditory and with visual learners. The auditory student will *hear* the rhyme of:

at: bat,   cat,   fat,   hat,   sat

The visual learner will *see* the gestalt of "at" and will apply the individual sound which precedes it. Another student might *associate* family words by making them into meaningful sentences to be remembered: "The fat cat with the hat sat on his bat." Making actual or mind pictures of this sentence facilitates the student's association of family words. The words in the picture should then be labeled not only by their design but also with the actual word.

Creative teaching needs to employ as many techniques as possible. There is a "bottom line" which is well known by families of children with learning and living difficulties: "If it works, do it!" The same is true in the classroom. The method by which one learns to read is far less critical than is the actual learning to read. Similarly, whether or not one reads every word, or every word correctly, can be incidental. The goal of reading is comprehension, or deriving meaning. Some people need to read every word, and read it correctly in order to understand what they have read. Others are able to skip one or several words in every sentence while comprehending perfectly adequately. Speed-reading courses are based on the idea of leaving words out, or of reading down the middle of the pages. All students are not capable of this advanced skill. Furthermore, one must be able to select the appropriate words to omit.

> "Mary had a little lamb" is better understood/more meaningful if one reads, "Mary - lamb" or "Mary had lamb," than if one chooses "had a little."

In this case, it is *not* the middle words that are the important ones.

For the most part, I very much support current models of teaching which utilize the reader/writer workshop schema, which include "conferencing" with students, and which advocate "publishing" student work. The myth, however, is that a whole language approach is "right for everyone." It has not been my experience that anything is right for everyone. Currently, in psychology and in education, "visualization" techniques are very much in vogue. Like whole language, visualization is tremendously useful for many, many people. It is a wonderful adjunct to relaxing, to learning, to memorizing; but it is not a worldwide panacea. On the one hand, I would strongly encourage teachers to become familiar with the work of Nanci Atwell, Donald Graves, Lucy Calkins, Georgia Heard, Jane Hansen, and others who teach through children's literature and through student work. On the other hand, I reiterate that there are some children who will need additional input or an alternative approach. In my practice, I see children who have had the very best exposure to language and literature. They are children of well-educated parents—children who have had fascinating life experiences. In spite of everything, they don't read, or they read beautifully and spell poorly. This fascinates me, and I feel continuously challenged to figure out new and alternative teaching methods to meet their needs.

For some few children, it is necessary to focus on drill and skill exercises. As an example of an instance when I might resort to this technique is the first-grade child who has not yet learned the home phone number and address. In today's world, this is such critical information that I would insist that a child practice and repeat the numbers until they are "automatized."

> I think of a first-grade child named Tom. Although Tom can sometimes recognize his name (which he sometimes refers to as Thomas even when it is Tom that he sees written), he is unable to remember how to spell Tom. Tom needs to see his name written all over everything at home. He needs to practice it over and over and over. Tom is a bright enough child; intellect is not an issue. Tom will do well in whole language programs where his conceptual abilities and his knowledge can enable him to contribute to class discussions and peer conversations. Nevertheless, he is seven years old and must be specifically taught to recognize letters, to spell his name, and to make the connections between letters and the words which they represent.

A few examples and suggestions of viable strategies for approaching students like Tom who experience language, reading, and writing delays are presented later in this chapter; but this is only a limited sample. Furthermore, the use of such strategies should be seen as an addition to language immersion, not as an alternative to it. Supplementary lessons in phonics, in visualization, in multisensory or kinesthetic involvements should take place several times a day for the child who needs additional, direct instruction. Like all children, these students will benefit by spending the main part of their day in rich language environments. The availability of books, student-written books included, cannot be overestimated. Some beginning readers like picture books that have no words so that they can make up their own stories and supply their own words rather than being stymied by those which already exist on the page. Other emerging readers enjoy hearing the same book over and over so that they can memorize the story and "read" it themselves. Most children love to hear and to read the stories of their classmates, and almost all children like best having their own stories "published." (Appendix B offers a literature resource list. The vast number of children's books makes it impossible to identify them individually; however, the resource list includes books which teach through literature and which show how to use specific books for particular lessons.)

Clearly, it is not my impression that a reading recipe occurs. For children who are struggling with reading and writing, basal readers continue to have some very strong points in their favor since there is something to be said for simplicity and repetition. While phonetic strategies often are quite successful for some students (particularly dyslexic students), children with hearing or auditory processing impairments frequently respond more favorably to a visual memory approach to learning to read. Usually multisensory tactics are invaluable, particularly in the classroom where one finds a variety of learners and learning styles. Language experience, whole language, and reading recovery programs tend to meet with substantial success among many students. Following is a list of some of the more traditional reading approaches, and an indication of which students can be helped most by these methods.

Phonics: Phonetic reading approaches (Orton-Gillingham, Slingerland) stress sound-symbol associations and sound blends. This can be a helpful approach for children with visual processing weaknesses. These programs work well with children who are good with sequential memory, and who benefit from a structured program which is broken into component tasks. Students who are weak sequentially or auditorily have difficulty with this approach.

Basal Readers: The traditional Scott-Foresman or Houghton Mifflin programs which are used in most elementary schools are made up of sequenced materials with vocabularies which are structured. The programs emphasize reading for meaning, and are effective with children who have good language and visual perception strategies. They are difficult for youngsters who struggle with attention deficits and language or visual perception problems because of the amount of material which must be attended to simultaneously.

Language Experience Programs: This approach emphasizes the child's own language experience and vocabulary. It integrates the teaching of listening, speaking, reading, and writing so that a coordinated process of "language" is presented. A child who experiences global language difficulties benefits from this kind of program, while the child who needs a very structured, well-defined program does not.

Linguistics: Phonemically regular words and word families are emphasized in these reading programs. Since sound patterns are the focus, children with good oral language do well in linguistic approaches, while children with weaknesses in processing whole words do not.

Multisensory Programs: The approach advocated in multisensory teaching is that of combining visual/auditory/kinesthetic and tactile modes of teaching. Most children do well with this strategy; however, some children with rather circumscribed and well-defined strengths and weaknesses may not. Those youngsters who are particularly strong in one modality and weak in the others may profit more by capitalizing on the strength. (Listed under Phonics, because it does emphasize phonetics, Slingerland is actually a multisensory approach.)

STRATEGIES FOR ACCOMMODATING SPECIFIC WEAKNESSES

Visual-Spatial Organization

Children who experience difficulties in visual-spatial organization may be those who manifest directional confusions. They can be youngsters who, from an early age, have trouble matching, sorting, identifying objects in an array, and telling left from right. Later, they frequently reverse letters, numbers, words, and digits. Reading comprehension may be better than reading accuracy, and listening comprehension may be superior to silent reading comprehension. Handwriting is often problematic. Word recognition and sight vocabulary are usually delayed.

Children with these visual-spatial organization weaknesses respond favorably to language experience, whole language, and phonetically based reading methods. Encouraging the use of an underliner or file card marker when reading is helpful because it augments tracking abilities. A "window card" for early readers also has this effect, facilitating visual attention and avoiding visual distraction. Finger pointing can be a useful strategy. Books that have few words on a page will increase comprehension and minimize confusion. So will books with big print. Color coding or highlighting important words or groups of ideas can be useful. Older children who must deal with textbooks should be encouraged to look at the big bold print subtitles for generating paragraph meaning, ideas, and themes. These children must stop after reading each paragraph to paraphrase or just to jot down a few notes in the margins.

Spelling words need to be broken into component parts, and spelled orally. Tracing of letters is particularly helpful when these children are young, and writing on lined paper is mandatory. Dot-to-dot work is useful in the early years, and writing within prescribed boundaries (margins on a page) is important later on.

Students with visual-spatial weaknesses will read for meaning more effectively than they will read for word accuracy. Reading out loud is difficult. As these children move through school, spelling continues to be problematic and requires considerable practice. Copying from a chalkboard is terribly difficult and can be compensated for by providing copies or by asking another student to copy the material for the visually weaker child. Eventually, a tape recorder becomes an important adjunct, as do typewriters and computers (with spell checks!).

Sequencing

Students with sequencing weaknesses have difficulty processing successive information. They are children who mix up concepts of "before and after," "earlier and later," and "now and then." They often learn to tell time much later than their peers, or they rely exclusively on digital clocks. They have trouble following spoken directions (which can frustrate parents and teachers). They will struggle with memorizing days of the week, months of the year, the order of the seasons, telephone numbers, and math sequences. Retelling stories or jokes goes poorly for these children—who may tell the punch line first! Recalling details and themes is problematic.

The ability to sound out words may develop more quickly than the ability to understand what is read. Answering specific questions may be significantly easier than retelling the story, which requires ordering the events. Spelling words may be accurately recognized as correct or incorrect, but retrieval spelling may be quite flawed. Written work is likely to be laboriously slow.

In the early years, one will want to focus on sequential ordering of pictures, objects, calendar sequences, and time. Sorting silverware and setting the table are particularly good exercises for little ones. Putting things next to each other according to categories (size, color, shapes) is helpful. The use of the calendar to notice and mark specific and sequential events becomes increasingly important. One might note the child's birthday, and then count the days (not more than four or five for young children, perhaps a week for kindergarten children), having the child count and mark off each day. Parents and teachers of children with sequencing difficulties should save many old calendars and use them for practicing days, months, seasons, groups of days, various time periods, or special events. The child always must be actively involved in marking whatever sequence is to be learned. Timers and clocks (analog) are other important teaching aids in this category of deficits. The sense of time—how much a certain period of time takes, and what happens before and after that amount of time—needs to be taught. Memorizing rhymes which pertain to sequential order (Thirty days has September, The Alphabet Song, Today Is Monday, and so on) can be useful. Mnemonic strategies are good as children get older.

Reading approaches which avoid memorization for sequential information are best. Phonetic blends are particularly difficult for these students. Teachers will want to integrate other approaches, emphasizing context clues and picture cues in the word decoding task. Reading for meaning is difficult because sequential material is not processed readily. It is good to stop frequently and ask the child to paraphrase or to tell back what was read, and ask how that fits into the main idea. "What just happened?" and "What do you think might happen next? Why?" are good questions for these students to be asked, and to learn to ask themselves.

Visual presentation and color coding of component parts of words are good spelling methods for children with sequential weaknesses. The learning and recognizing of frequently used prefixes and suffixes will be useful in spelling and in essay writing. Written work may not be as noticeably problematic in the early grades as it is in late elementary school when there is an increased demand for writing sentences and paragraphs, and for organizing thoughts and ideas on paper. Sequencing difficulties often manifest themselves in mathematics because it is important to place numbers in the correct spot or order, and because regrouping requires sequential organization. Word problems, algebra, and geometry depend upon sequential understanding and sequential memory.

Language Processing

Children with communication problems often do not fall into readily defined categories and may display a tremendously wide range and variety of school difficulties. It is complicated because students with speech impairments or with auditory processing weaknesses may not have language delays; while the child with language deficits may have no trouble with speech, and could be strong in auditory processing. At home and at school language-delayed children may be difficult to understand and may have trouble understanding. They often do not like to answer questions and have trouble finding the words they want to use. They may be limited in their group involvement both socially and academically, and they are frequently distracted by irrelevant noises or are startled by unusual sounds. These children have trouble listening and attending, so they tire easily. Often they are mistaken for attention-deficit youngsters. Following instructions is almost always problematic for the language-impaired child. Since their day-to-day language environment is taxing and confusing, a predictable and consistent routine is especially helpful.

Although most children with auditory language difficulties need to practice phonetic material, it is not an easy way for them to learn to read. A considerable amount of language experience which connects a child's knowledge with reading will be more meaningful. An integrated learning experience will enhance reading and writing skills for children with language delays. The more they can relate words to categories, to their own lives, to other people's lives, the better; particularly so because they struggle with reading comprehension. It is important to relate words to their meaning and to their utility. Teaching these children to read and to write the words which they need in their daily lives is helpful.

Language intervention is most effective when it occurs throughout the day rather than in a pull-out program for an hour or so. Children with listening and communicating difficulties must be immersed in language, albeit in short doses with frequent "rest periods." Language exhausts them, but it cannot be avoided and must be brought into all parts of the child's day. The sound-symbol associations which cause them so much difficulty need to be emphasized throughout their day in order for them to become ready to read and to write. Family words and words with similar spelling patterns are good ones to practice. Language-delayed children who are strong visually should be encouraged to draw upon that strength in making associations between words and pictures. Children who have good memorizing skills will benefit from constant repetition and exposure to word configuration. A multisensory approach to reading and writing is an especially good technique with children having language-processing dysfunctions.

As children get older, the "cloze" method is a particularly helpful approach to comprehension, reading, and writing. This procedure involves a sentence in which one or more words is deleted. The student is required to fill in the missing word, which necessitates the student's understanding the meaning of the sentence, recalling the word the student wants to use, saying or writing the word, and perhaps generating several possible words. For young students, if a particular word is requested, the beginning and/or end letter could be supplied. For older students, the possibility of a variety of words may be more broadening. Also, leaving out several sentences or a whole passage can stimulate good thinking.

To enhance reading comprehension, the student may be asked questions about the text which are inferential or, at least, which are not answered directly in the material read. Important words, or common words, may be isolated for spelling lists or for using in other sentences. Writing words is good for reinforcing the memorization of them.

GENERAL STRATEGIES FOR THE SLOWER LEARNER

Although specific learning delays may respond better or worse to particular reading/writing approaches, there are some children who, for no obvious reasons, simply emerge as readers and writers a little more slowly than their peers. They may have mild weaknesses which are not readily identified, or they may manifest "soft-sign" neurological dysfunctions which impede their progress at a "normal" rate. Most of the strategies outlined above serve all children in the classroom quite well, even though some students need them more specifically than do others. In general, most young children benefit from structure and organization in the classroom and at home. Consistency and predictability are good prescriptions for almost every young child. Similarly, almost all students profit from a multisensory approach to learning. Teaching which actively involves the child in the learning process has proven to be highly successful.

Reading and writing require an understanding of language and sight/sound-symbol relationships; therefore, preschool and kindergarten children need to practice acting out and drawing out their lives. They need to be taught to listen and to express themselves and their needs in meaningful ways. Both oral and motoric (sign language, body language) communication should be encouraged, helping children to become expressive and receptive in these skills. Helping young children to name and to label their pictures, to tell and to write their stories, and to connect letters with words and words with pictures facilitates their reading/writing readiness.

As children move into the early grades, it is important to continue to pay attention to developmental stages, engaging children in academic learning which is relevant to their cognitive and affective level of development. (Teachers need to have a good understanding of early child development.) Most children continue to benefit from the use of manipulatives, active involvement, and discovery learning. High-interest-level material augments the desire and the ability to read and to write. Continued activities with directionality and sequencing are crucial for the language arts. Small groups, cooperative learning techniques, structure, teacher involvement, offering new material in small pieces and relating new material to previous knowledge, group discussions, and breaking directions, tasks, and words into component parts have all been found to benefit young students. Children need to be read to in order to become readers; they need to be exposed to their own and other students' writing if they are going to become writers.

In general, as was discussed earlier, the slower learners do not spontaneously apply strategies for reading and writing which would be helpful for them. For instance, most school textbooks are relatively cluttered with words and are difficult to manage. Children who do not automatically sort out the material on the page must be taught how to do so. The child needs to be told to look at boldface print, to read headings and sub-headings, to relate portions to the whole, and to read picture captions. The primary goal is to teach the child how to draw his attention to the most important material and to focus on the specific theme, or on the problem to be solved.

Emerging readers and writers need to know to begin on the left side of the page. A bright star, sticker, or arrow could highlight the left side to accentuate it as the starting point. Giving the child the marker or sticker and asking, "Where are you going to put this to let you know the place to begin?" involves the child and increases awareness. Specific colors to code directionality of letters/numbers, highlighters to emphasize thematic material or important information, window boxes to isolate words or phrases in reading, looking at picture clues, titles, big bold print, contents, summaries, and indexes are strategies which do not appear to be obvious to children with learning delays.

Teachers will want to make both oral and written directions as concise and uncomplicated as possible. Lengthy descriptions should be avoided since too many words, either auditorily or visually, get in the way. Providing many different occasions and kinds of opportunities to use language and to hear language will facilitate the reading and writing processes. Letters, journals, and diaries often appeal to young children more than reports or essays. Books which have particular pertinence to a child's life or magazine articles about a favorite sport or hobby can be enticing. Flexibility and a willingness to be open to a wide variation in learning styles will enable the teacher to meet with greater success. It is not possible to overemphasize the advantages of a sensitive teacher who can recognize and celebrate the strengths of each child; yet, one who can appreciate as well the difficulties each child experiences so that these too can be understood and remediated. Since no one is perfect, all students and teachers have strengths and weaknesses which can be integrated into the classroom development. Teacher attention, positive peer relationships, and individual integrity contribute to successful learning in every classroom.

A SCENARIO

It is difficult to construct an isolated sample lesson because whatever is devised will be out of context, and will address certain needs, while leaving out others. Nevertheless, I have tried to show, in one small, specific way, an example of how a teacher might put together a lesson which is for the whole class but which will also incorporate the individual needs of several different learning strengths and weaknesses. Imagine the following script:

The title of the play (goal of the lesson) is Facts and Feelings.

The class has made a decision to spend the week learning about zoos. They have cut out pictures of animals that belong in a zoo; they have labeled these animals; they have made pictures and clay figures of various animals and their habitats (new vocabulary word); and they have collected many books about animals and zoos from the school library.

It is Thursday, four days into the zoo theme. The teacher decides that during the language arts hour, she would like to focus on helping children to understand the difference between *facts* and *feelings*. The teacher is the director of this lesson, and the students become the players.

In preparing for class, the teacher remembers that there are several children who have been having trouble with putting anything down on paper this week because they were spending most of their time playing with clay and making animal noises. She writes down these four names and decides to ask each of them to be the "recorder" in their cooperative groups. Then she recalls that two of the boys were especially interested in lions. These two students often have trouble working in groups, so the teacher will ask them to work together on a special project to see if they can find and record six facts about where lions live and how they get their food. She will show them how to use an encyclopedia. In this class, there are a number of children who seem to have difficulty visualizing what they are reading or hearing, and they tend not to remember information very well. The teacher decides to sit one of them next to each recorder, and will give them the job of illustrator, asking them to make a picture of each fact that the recorder writes down.

The teacher is not sure just what some of the other children will want to do. She has several thoughts in mind, but she will wait until the lesson evolves, watching for what seems to spark them, and asking them what part of the fact/feeling project interests them.

At the beginning of this class, the children sit on the floor facing the teacher. She says: "I am going to tell you some things about me. I want you to listen for the things which tell you about how I feel, and I want you to pay attention to some facts which tell you about me, but they are not my feelings. Listen to see if you can figure this out. I have blue eyes and brown hair. I am happy today. I have three children of my own. I like teaching this class."

The teacher allows for some class discussion. Then she asks two volunteers to write some information on the chalkboard. Sammy comes up to the chalkboard, and the teacher writes the heading "Facts" on her left side. Sophie stands on her right, where she writes "Feelings." The teacher asks the other children to say some things about themselves which are facts or feelings, and the class decides whether they belong on Sammy's side or Sophie's side.

After a few minutes, the teacher tells the class that they are going to be in small groups which she will assign, and she will want each group to talk about animal facts and animal feelings. She has put three books on each table which they may use if they want. Each group will have a recorder and an illustrator. She wonders if they have ideas about roles for other members. The children suggest that the groups should have two book readers and one person who will share with the whole class afterward what was said in their group.

Before dividing them into groups, the teacher talks to them a minute more about seeing in their heads each animal they discuss, and thinking about painting a mind-picture of that animal. Then she says that a fact is easier to see and to draw than a feeling. "I can draw two eyes better than I can draw scared," she says, "but I can feel inside of me what scared is like."

As the groups meet, the teacher walks around the classroom chatting with individual children and with each group. She notices that Jeremy does not seem to be very invested in his group work, and asks him if he has something special on his mind. Jeremy says that his cat died the night before, and he doesn't want to think about feelings. His teacher recognizes his sadness, and invites him to make up names for each of the animals the class has labeled for their zoo. Jeremy walks from cage to cage in the room writing down made-up names — and then he writes a story about some of these animals and how they want to get out of their cages. Later on, the teacher will have him read his story and will ask the class to identify the feelings which Jeremy has given to his animals.

As the teacher passes Ann's desk, she sees that Ann is writing the feeling words in all capital letters. The teacher comments that Ann must find the feelings very important in that she is making them all so big. Ann giggles, and says, "No." The teacher asks Ann if she could write all the happy, wonderful feelings in uppercase letters and all the sad, awful feelings in lowercase letters. The group decides to help Ann choose which ones are which.

Twenty minutes later, the teacher reconvenes the class. The representatives are given two minutes each to tell what happened in their groups. (A timer is used and is monitored by Seth, who often has trouble sitting still during circle times.) The teacher says quietly, "I am tired from all of this work." Several children shout out: "Feeling!" Then the teacher asks if someone will stand and tell the class the most interesting fact he or she learned. Many hands go up.

The teacher closes this lesson by telling the class that the world is full of facts and feelings. She asks them if they would go home and think about facts and feelings they see in their own families, and she suggests that they might want to write some of those observations down in their journals—just in case they may need a writing idea tomorrow during reading/writing workshop....

The point to be emphasized is that the teacher really only needed to make one lesson plan, but a number of mini-agendas existed within the big picture. Individual needs were met at the same time that everyone learned something about the fact/feeling lesson goal. Many children were given the opportunity to learn in a manner which was comfortable for them and some were asked to work on skills which needed more practice. Everyone participated. Teachers benefit from offering this type of learning experience because each student becomes involved in the most creative and contributory way possible for that child.

SUMMARY: IDENTIFYING OR RECOGNIZING LANGUAGE DYSFUNCTIONS

When several of the following conditions co-exist, consider a language-based deficit. Rarely will one issue alone suggest a language disorder.

POSSIBLE INDICATIONS

A child:

- frequently misuses common words

- consistently mispronounces many words or words with certain letters or letter combinations

- has trouble recalling everyday words

- hesitates for a long time before answering

- often seems confused by directions or instructions

- has trouble conveying needs or messages

- chooses nonverbal activities virtually all of the time

- mixes up words in a sentence

- is fussy during story time or silent-reading time

- never volunteers to do oral reporting

- shows, but doesn't tell

- finds conversation aversive or confusing

- does not engage in subvocalized or conversational play

- often misunderstands or does not understand academically and/or socially

- spells most words incorrectly most of the time

- does not understand rhyming or mnemonic strategies

WHAT TO DO

Observe and describe the student who is having difficulties.

A miscue or some similar notation of the child's reading errors may be appropriate.

Analyze the child's spelling errors. Is there a pattern to the mistakes?

Decide whether a referral may be useful—either to the special ed resource people in the school building or to an outside specialist.

Have a talk with the student, and with the parents, about your recognition of the difficulties. Ask for their input.

Consider a multisensory approach to teaching.

Use compensatory strategies in teaching so that the visually weak child will have plenty of oral instruction and many opportunities to perform orally; while the child with auditory deficits will be given written directions, a partner to help, and more time to write.

The child with fine motor weaknesses can compensate by learning to use a keyboard or typewriter, a tape recorder for recording reports and answers, and partner or group situations in which someone else does the writing.

Dyslexic students usually need some outside remediation, but can be helped by color codes, phonetic instruction, tactile input, and a partner. They need a lot of one-to-one attention, but it does not always need to be the teacher who provides it.

Students with visual-spatial organization difficulties need few words on a page, window cards, color codes, underliners for reading and for highlighting. Learning to outline and to paraphrase are helpful strategies. They should *not* be asked to copy from a board or book. Use lined and graph paper. Use computers and tape recorders.

Sequential weaknesses in young children require considerable practice with lining things up, categorizing, grouping, and ordering of objects and of ideas. Talk about what happens first, next, last. What is in the middle? What happened after that? Do not expect good storytelling or good recall of the events in the stories.

Children with sequential difficulties have trouble with spelling, and should be taught to memorize the most commonly used words. They should use Franklin Spellers, and should have a parent or peer help with editing their written work.

Students with memory deficits require a heavy dose of a multisensory approach so that all of their senses contribute to the remembering process. They need constant review and many reminders. Use many strategies and devices which will facilitate remembering. Silly tricks, rhymes, songs, and pleasantries often help.

Language-delayed children may do better with silent reading and reading comprehension rather than stressing reading out loud or retelling of stories. Some may do better with written work, but many do not. Try it to see.

REFERENCE LIST

Bloom, L., and M. Lahey. (1978) *Language Development and Language Disorders*. New York: Wiley.

Chall, Jeanne S. (1983) *Stages of Reading Development*. New York: McGraw-Hill.

Fitzgerald, J. (1951) *A Basic Life Spelling Vocabulary*. Milwaukee, WI: Bruce.

Kraus, Robert. (1971) *Leo the Late Bloomer*. New York: Windmill Books.

Palincsar, A. S., and A. L. Brown. (1984) Reciprocal teaching of comprehension—fostering and monitoring activities. *Cognition and Instruction* 1: 117-75.

Piaget, J. (1962) *The Language and Thought of the Child*. New York: World Publishing.

Uzgiris, Ina C., and J. McV. Hunt. (1975) *Assessment in Infancy*. Urbana, IL: University of Illinois Press.

Vygotsky, L. (1962) *Thought and Language*. Cambridge, MA: MIT Press.

6

Teaching and Learning Mathematics

Why don't you pair 'em up in threes?

Ninety-nine percent of this game is half mental!
—Yogi Berra

Subtract—regroup. I think this is the kind of deal where you cross out these top numbers.

Yea! That's subtraction; I think you do that in subtraction.

But now what?
—Two third graders

I had a boy in my class who came from a disadvantaged home. He had almost no experience using numbers. Kyle was having a hard time keeping up with the class until we began doing a unit on "scale drawings." I took out rulers, tape measures, yardsticks, and pieces of string. We were planning to do a scale model of our classroom, but Kyle, who was very artistic, all of a sudden began to understand addition, and putting numbers together started to make sense to him; so, he took out colored chalk and measured and drew all over the school. He added sides to original pieces of paper, and planned for spaces between the classrooms; he measured parts of walls and floors, and added those in

---

This chapter was written with Ronald E. Ritchhart.

too. Pretty soon, Kyle had made us a model of the whole school. I had been thinking about teaching Kyle subtraction, but then I assumed he had probably figured it all out.
—Third-grade teacher

THE CONCEPT OF NUMERACY

Mathematics is a symbolic language, and a system which allows for the recording of many events in daily living. While arithmetic represents only computational operations, mathematics covers the entire fabric of numbers and numerical relationships and, thus, has broad implications which stretch far beyond classroom academics. Recently, John Allen Paulos (1988) wrote about "innumeracy," the mathematical equivalent to illiteracy, and suggested that severe impairments in the conceptualization and appreciation of number concepts are as debilitating in today's world as is the inability to read or write. Mathematical literacy, or *numeracy*, which has gained increased attention in the technological age of the past several decades, is dependent upon not only a sense of numbers, but also on "ability to handle mathematical concepts such as chance, logic, and statistics. Like literacy, numeracy involves the ability to read and interpret information: quantitative information" (Ritchhart 1991, p. 6).

Unfortunately, it is quite common for a sizable number of students to experience some difficulty in school mathematics. Too often, the approach to the teaching of mathematics is disconnected from students' lives and interests. For many, school mathematics becomes a series of pointless exercises which lack meaning and relevance. The students who struggle in the classroom, however, may demonstrate considerable talent in employing mathematics in real-life situations. They may be able to manage time, budget money, and make a continuous stream of estimates and mental calculations in their daily lives. These students may not lack mathematical talent or understanding, but their teachers have failed to exploit their talents.

However, other students, those who do have difficulties with number concepts or with quantitative thinking, are likely to experience many daily living problems—problems which become increasingly frustrating and interfering as one gets older and looks toward independent living. A sense of time, of order, of distance, and of quantity are critical to one's ability to function independently. Students who are confused about numerical relationships and who cannot apply mathematical principles and problems to real-life situations are likely to lead their lives rigidly and without much variation. They buy apples because they know how much apples cost, while the cost of peaches may alter their grocery bill; they take the five-o'clock bus because they are not sure how to figure out when an earlier or later bus arrives; they always drive the same route to work even though a friend points out that there is a shortcut which would allow for 10 extra minutes of sleep in the mornings. Students with numeracy dysfunctions often grow into adults who are unable to make time, schedule, or money adjustments; who do not travel much because they cannot figure out how to get where they want to go; or who do not show much flexibility in daily life planning.

As early as the 1950s, Inhelder stated that "A child's ability to write a correct answer is not a valid objective in arithmetic" (Introduction, p. vii, in Kamii 1985). She was referring to the importance of the student's understanding of why and how the student arrived at the answer. Today's focus on problem solving de-emphasizes skill in arithmetic computation and places more importance on numerical context, relationship, probability, and conceptualization. Increasingly, children must learn to deal with numbers in measurement (distance in space, complex building constructs), in estimation (people at concerts, donations needed, cooking for large groups), and in chance (disasters, lotteries). While number lines, rulers, charts, tables, and calculators can facilitate accuracy in the arithmetic portion of problems, there is no tool which can substitute for the conceptualization and awareness of the meaning of the numbers involved. Therefore, it is important to have at least some understanding of numerical concepts: a horse is 13 hands; a basketball is what I can put my arms around; a 10-pound bag of sugar is what I can lift; one minute is how long it takes me to read a page of a book I like.

John Holt (1989) advised that children should "first meet numbers as adjectives, not nouns ... two coins, three matches, four forks ..." (p. 47). Although Holt felt that children should not be taught to count number names in the absence of real numbers, many early educators would disagree with him. The rote counting sequence is a language acquisition activity for young children. The task for teachers and students is to connect the counting sequence to meaningful experiences with numbers so that the child comes to understand both the cardinal and ordinal nature of numbers. As such, the counting sequence serves as a starting place for such activities. We make a mistake if we assume rote counting is an indicator of number understanding. Kamii (1985) also has emphasized the need to allow children to experience numbers; however, she has devised many games for young children that are predicated upon rote counting and that promote an understanding of number concepts. Kamii contends that a conceptual appreciation of numeracy evolves from participating with numbers in meaningful activities rather than through textbook teaching.

An example of a game which can be used at different levels in a classroom math lesson, as suggested by Kamii, utilizes the commercially made game of Parcheesi®. Each player selects one of the four colors and begins by placing four markers of that color in the corresponding circle. The object of the game is to move all four of a player's markers around the board to Home. Instead of playing with the usual dice, Kamii uses a single 10-sided die with the numerals 1 to 10 on each side. For beginning number students, the amount indicated can be that which is moved; but more advanced students will have fun by doubling the number shown and advancing that number of spaces. This game can be further extended by requiring a player to go back to the beginning if the player lands on the same space as another player. Children who are moving along quickly in their conceptualization of numbers will begin to strategize about how to send other players back and how to keep from being sent back themselves. For instance, one might figure out that a distance of 20 spaces between two players' markers is necessary in order not to be sent back. Those students who are playing at an earlier level also will enjoy playing the game. When they are ready to move ahead, it is likely that they will devise a new game on their own, or that a slight suggestion from their teacher will spark them to create a new rule or strategy for making their game more challenging, drawing on more advanced mathematical concepts. This very simple yet adaptable game provides students the opportunity to practice the counting sequence while establishing one-to-one correspondence, to connect numerals with their number meaning, and to count on and develop simple strategies.

Ritchhart (1991) proposes that mathematics involves investigative learning, which is an approach to finding out more about a problem or situation. "Investigations move students beyond problem solving to a state of problem posing," which is important because students "can build on their prior knowledge by exploring questions which are important to them as individuals" (p. 17). As was discussed in the previous chapter, it is usually one's knowledge base which offers the construction of meaning and the development of relevance and understanding. However, it also is true that some people seem to "see" things mathematically:

> I think of mathematics almost as observations. There is somehow a mathematical world which is really there. Certain patterns in it fit together in certain ways. It is just a question of learning to see what they are.
> — Bill Thurston, Princeton University

Giving a child the opportunity to make investigations into numerical problem solving enriches the student's prior experience with number concepts. At home and in preschool, there are continuous possibilities for allowing this to happen. Much of a young child's way of thinking and conversing, in fact, is very number-specific: "She has *more* than I do," "There are not *enough* crayons for *all* of us," "His is *bigger* than mine," "We will go in *10 minutes*," "Wait for me *before* you go out" are among the many examples of mathematical concepts we hear parents, teachers, and children using in everyday conversations.

In their own subtle (and not so subtle) ways, young children constantly investigate alternative strategies and solutions to problems: "If I do this, then what will happen?" "What happens next?" "What if I do not do this or that?" "If such-and-such happens once, will it happen again? Will it always happen the same way?" and so on. These are questions involving probability, constancy, averaging, estimating, deducing, and so forth. Questions such as these are the ones which children must be given time to pursue and to explore as they move through the educational process. At various points in their own development and in their own learning, children will approach these types of questions differently because they are questions about numeracy, on the one hand, and about life on the other. The understanding of their outcome depends upon one's past experience, knowledge, perspective, and cognitive ability. Investigative learning allows for question-posing and for trial-and-error experiences. A teacher must not feel the need to teach for mastery. Rather, the goals can be oriented toward exposure, toward making numbers meaningful and interesting, and toward the teacher's own improvement as a resource person.

Students with specific learning disabilities may struggle hard to arrive at viable solutions to mathematical dilemmas. Computational skills can be especially difficult for children with sequencing deficits or with visual-perceptual weaknesses. Conceptual understanding may be elusive for the child who experiences language delays. Memory dysfunctions will certainly impede a student's progress in arithmetic skills and in the development of numeracy concepts. Children having spatial relationship problems may memorize math facts flawlessly, but will write them inaccurately, while students with visual-perceptual disturbances may toil over acquiring computational skills even though the concepts are clear to them. Even though these children do poorly on math tests in school, one can appreciate their conceptual skills by observing them in their daily living. They are the young children who know immediately that if four friends are sick, there are 20, not 24, children in class that day. They may understand that half the class wants orange juice and the other half wants milk. Older children may do well on oral math tests; they may excel when there is a math or spelling

The Concept of Numeracy ■ 83

bee; they will know how to judge the time it will take them to walk or to drive to school given the distance that must be travelled. This is different from the child who has not been able to conceptualize these everyday problems. The latter, for instance, would not allow a longer period of time to walk to school than to drive there. For that child, school is 15 minutes away from home, "My mother told me so!"

Temporal or visual-sequential deficits usually manifest themselves early in a child's life, and they almost always have a substantial impact on the child's mathematical learning. Parents recognize the three-year-old who frequently is confused by directionality, looking under the bed rather than on the bed, going upstairs instead of downstairs, walking out the front door when meaning to go to the backyard, having trouble with learning to dress themselves or to be in a new place. These are youngsters who cannot seem to understand concepts of up/down, more/less, under/over, before/after, near/far, here/there. "Tomorrow I went to the movie" is not a grammatical error, but a temporal misunderstanding for six-year-old Jen. Conversation with Jen is often confusing because of her temporal disorganization. "Are we going to go before now?" "When will it be yesterday?" "Can I sit in front of the front seat?" "You said to end at the start." These are the kinds of mis-messages this child sends and receives. While they appear to be language-based difficulties, and in some sense they are, they actually are more sequential dysfunctions which have important implications vis-à-vis her mathematical development.

Place value concepts, including regrouping, are significantly difficult concepts for students having sequential confusions. Place value often has little meaning; it is not unusual for the child to subtract as follows:

$$
\begin{array}{ccc}
22 & & 22 \\
-14 & \text{or} & -14 \\
\hline
16 & & 12
\end{array}
$$

In the first instance, 6 is acquired by adding 4 + 2; whereas in the second example, 2 is arrived at by taking 2 away from 4. Not having regrouped, the child then subtracts 1 from 2 and puts down the 1. While this is commonly observed among children in the early stages of learning to subtract, the child with learning difficulties may continue to make such errors well into grade school.

```
    32
  - 17
  ────
    25
```

While a rose is always a rose, a two is not always a two; as is seen in the example above wherein one two is a two (but through regrouping it becomes a 12 while the other is regrouped into two 10s or a 20). The following two's are read as two, twenty, two hundred, and two hundred twenty-two:

      2   20   200   222

Clearly, place value can be extremely confusing for the child who does not have a strong sense of numbers.

Place value also is complicated for children experiencing visual-spatial organization weaknesses because they may misperceive the alignment of the columns or positions of numbers so that a 32 may be processed as a 23; a 6 for a 9; or even an F for a 7. Students with visual-spatial organization weaknesses may do less accurate work with paper and pencil than they do orally; however, this may not be the case, and they will do equally ineffective work whether it is written or spoken, even though they can understand the concepts being discussed. While the answers will come out wrong, the method or process required to arrive at an answer will make sense to the student. For instance, the child knows to subtract, but arrives at an incorrect result.

In helping these children, it is useful to use graph paper so that they can align the numbers in their proper columns. Sometimes, color coding the graph paper is necessary. The fewer the number of problems on a page, the better because there is a visual overload when rows and rows of problems are in front of the child. Copying from the chalkboard or out of the book — not a useful plan for any student — will almost certainly cause errors and usually requires an exorbitant amount of time for children with various learning difficulties, particularly those who have trouble with perception, fine motor skills, or organization.

Children with language difficulties are less hampered in computational skills than they are with word problems. While these youngsters may do well with computational problems, they will look less accomplished as their math becomes increasingly involved with reading and writing. It may be hard for them to conceptualize higher-level problem-solving tasks or to generalize from one problem situation to another even though their math facts are well established.

Generalizing, or making connections, is an important aspect of mathematics. Without connections, students become burdened by memorizing isolated facts and principles rather than conceptualizing broad ideas which can be applied in various problem-solving situations. Teachers need to facilitate the making of connections, as they do not often happen spontaneously. Questions which encourage children to identify similarities and differences among concepts, ideas, and activities are useful in this respect. Good instruction enables children to appreciate the relationships between manipulatives and the symbols and concepts which they represent. Teachers will want to help children see the relationships among the various content strands of mathematics, and between math and other academic areas. Connecting mathematics to other disciplines offers students the opportunity to understand math's real-life usefulness, and affords meaningful applications of mathematical skills. Grocery store shopping has become the most practical example of this need, as it is very typical for LD adults to collect $60 worth of groceries in their carts when they only have $20 in their pocket.

Whole language/language experience programs usually are associated with reading and writing, but, in fact, good whole language instruction does and should include mathematics in its teachings. "Whole mathematics" should involve reading and writing with a numerical emphasis. Journal writing can foster mathematical learning.

> Today we were putting numbers into groups of things. I love to do these kinds of things, but I got frustrated because I couldn't think of anything for 11. I had 1 unicorn horn, 2 beats in a measure, 3 lights on a stop-light, 4 heads on Mount Rushmore, all the way up until 9, which I couldn't think of; but the teacher said 9 lives of a cat. I'm still thinking about something for 11. I hope I get it before Molly does.
> —Third-grade girl

> We read a story about a candy store near a train station. It had a problem because the candy bags kept tearing, so everyone's candy fell out all over the train. We were supposed to design some sort of candy container which would hold just the right amount of candy and be strong so the stuff wouldn't fall out. There were supposed to be different-size boxes for different amounts of candy pieces. I got stuck on this because I couldn't figure out how to put 29 pieces evenly in the box since there

weren't any numbers which did this evenly. It wasn't about odd numbers because I got 25 pieces in five rows of five, but I couldn't get the 29. I've been thinking a lot about this problem. Maybe I need to talk about it with my teacher.

—Fourth-grade boy

Many times, sixth-, seventh-, and eighth-grade students cannot describe what it is that they are "doing" in math class. It is astonishing how few children are able to describe linguistically the mathematical processes and concepts with which they are working on a daily basis. Sometimes a student can say, "We are working on fractions" (decimals or volume), but not frequently. Moreover, too few students can go beyond that, even when asked pertinent questions such as "Why do we need to know about fractions?" "Why is understanding about volume important?" "When do you think you might want to find the area of a place?" "How would understanding about graphs be helpful to you?"

Recently, a very bright third grader told his teacher, "Perimeters are deceiving!" This child was investigating lengths, widths, and distances around with a piece of string equal to his own height. He discovered that perimeters were "usually bigger" than he had anticipated them to be. Another third grader in the same class, however, was unable to make the connection between the string's length, the student's height, and the distance around a box. This child had not yet attained conservation of length, and was unable to recognize that the box was the same number of inches around as the child was tall. Although the second child has been able to memorize addition and subtraction facts, the numbers do not yet have practical meaning and application to this student.

Developing one-to-one correspondence is a first step in making this kind of connection. A child must be able to match rote number sequences with the counting of actual, concrete objects. The numbers need to take on meaning so that a child understands that three apples are not the same as four apples, and that numbers can be counted in sequence to find out "how many." "It is much more important for the child to learn to move his or her finger from one object to the next as he or she counts than to simply say the numbers" (Johnson-Martin, et al. 1990). It is often useful for young children to become involved with many games which have kinesthetic cues for learning number concepts. For example, walking through the number line as opposed to simply counting through it may be helpful for children who have trouble with spatial or visual awareness. Understanding that 2 is closer to 3 than it is to 8 may make more sense to the child if the child walks down a line of 10 children rather than looking at the numbers across the chalkboard.

Many preschool teachers use snack time as an additional opportunity to understand one-to-one correspondence: pass out one cup for each child, one napkin for each child, and so on. Some children will realize that one cracker and one celery stick can go at each place, but they will be confused if told to give two cookies to each person. (Two cookies at one place?!) Counting various classroom materials (blocks, crayons, balls, and so on) reinforces one-to-one correspondence. Stringing beads, placing pegs in holes, clapping, jumping, and sorting while counting all facilitate the counting principle. While most young children enjoy counting (and saying the alphabet) — they often have races to see who can do it the fastest or the longest, or the most — and while these informal games are excellent for reinforcing number/letter sequences, the association of number names to number of things may not get established if actual, concrete manipulatives are not used. Motor-based activities aid in the conceptual development of one-to-one correspondence.

The concept of seriation is a cornerstone component of a student's mathematical learning. Again, the sorting and selecting activities are those which contribute to mastery of this concept. Big/little and more/less seem to come into play most frequently in the preschool classroom as children make comparisons between themselves and others. Stories which incorporate size and number are good adjuncts. *Goldilocks*, for example, has one girl, three bears, and "too big" used repetitively. *The Big Fat Enormous Lie* involves a "lie" which grows bigger and bigger, then smaller and smaller. *Changes, Changes* is a wonderful picture book which shows how the same number and size blocks can be used to make various designs. This reinforces the idea of number "invariance" or constancy: no matter how the blocks are arranged, there are still the same number of blocks.

Children having certain visual perceptual dysfunctions often spend a long time mastering the learning of size, shape, and quantity. In fact, they may conceptually understand the idea of one-to-one correspondence, of groups of objects, or of more/less concepts, but they have trouble "seeing" it. At the early stages of learning, it is helpful to use different-colored objects. Six blue cars may be more complicated than six different-colored cars. "The orange car is bigger than the blue car." "The red truck has more wheels than the yellow race car." Shifting the arrangement of the cars from lines to circles to triangles while keeping the number of cars constant will make more sense to the child if the child does the manipulating rather than looking at pictures of these designs or configurations. Tactile input is particularly useful for children with visualization and memory difficulties. Color coding also can facilitate their learning.

As children move into the early years of elementary school, they will begin to deal with concepts of place value. Grouping objects together is an important part of their understanding of this process. They need to work with objects which possess a one-to-one correspondence, with each object having a value equal to one. Students will explore these materials, making chains, trains, geometric designs, and other such groupings. Later, they will be ready to move on to materials possessing a predetermined structure and form, such as Cuisenaire® rods and base-ten blocks. When appropriate materials are used in the classroom, it becomes quite obvious to teachers which children are struggling with which numerical concepts. Until a child has mastered these "foundation" basics, it is not wise to push the child ahead arithmetically. The child may be able to memorize more advanced facts and figures, but if they do not make conceptual sense, the child will not be able to generalize them to new or similar situations. Some students with particular learning difficulties have trouble generalizing between what happens in math class and what occurs in their daily life. Teachers will want to use many practical examples for such students, constantly connecting what is being done in the classroom with a real and practical life experience.

For example, students should not associate "estimating" just with math class, but should come to understand when and why estimating may be useful to them in their lives. In fact, estimating may be one of the most important "math" concepts to teach children with learning delays because these are often children who seem to be weak in the areas of common sense and judgment. Learning how to make appropriate estimations is dependent upon one's understanding of conservation and is involved with cause-and-effect principles. Cause-and-effect implications frequently elude children with learning difficulties. Learning to make relatively reliable estimates rather than "wild guesses" is invaluable to children who experience language, sequencing, attentional, or socio-emotional weaknesses.

Children need to be made aware of the purpose of estimating, when it is used, how to estimate, and how to judge the appropriateness of an estimate. Estimating provides a framework for judging the reasonableness of answers, and this "range of reasonableness" should be emphasized continuously and in many different situations. How much juice one needs for a snack has a smaller range of reasonableness, for instance, than how many birds are in the aviary at the zoo.

Many metacognitive questions need to be introduced in order for a child to make appropriate estimates. As has been discussed earlier, children with various learning differences tend not to think much about their thinking and about the ways in which they approach problem solving; yet, they need these skills in so many aspects of their daily lives. Thinking about estimation is but one example of how one uses knowledge of and experience with numbers.

The amount of information one has is a major contributing factor in producing accurate estimates, whether one is in math class or on the playground. In order to make good estimates, children need to be taught to ask themselves the appropriate questions, utilizing their own knowledge base and experiences; otherwise they are making guesses, not estimates. An American child who is asked how many French francs will fit into a liter container can only guess and will not be able to make a reasonable estimation until told that a franc is about the size of a quarter and a liter is a little more than a quart. Learning to take samples, or to break problems down into smaller pieces, is a part of this process. In this same example, the student may make a more accurate estimate if told that there are about seven francs in one-fourth cup; or better yet, if the student is asked to experiment with measuring and counting in the "sampling" process. This experimentation and these "clues" enhance the student's ability to ask relevant questions and to make connections. The exact answer, of course, is much less important than is an appreciation of the "range of reasonableness" of one's estimation. (Very few life problems have exact answers.)

As an early identifier, it is often the children who have trouble with time, with stopping and starting, with boundaries, and with limits who manifest difficulties with estimation. These are the children who pour too much milk into their cereal bowl (daily), who do not slow down on their tricycles when they reach the corner or the end of the driveway, who need *all* of the clay or paint or blocks. Sharing is often difficult because they are poor at estimating what their needs really are. These characteristics can be confused with impulsivity and some of them, indeed, are the same; but for some children, it is not a question of not paying attention, but rather one of not being able to make appropriate judgments. It is very valuable to spend a lot of time with these youngsters taking actual samples of things (kernels of corn to make a box of popcorn, strokes across the width of a pool, people in one row at the movie theater, reactions to the telling of a joke) in order to reinforce concretely the basis of making an appropriate estimation, a skill which will facilitate their math and life opportunities.

Measuring is another mathematical concept which has many practical applications. Again, children need to see that measurement is done for a purpose. An understanding of size, volume, weight, width, length, height, and distance enables children to use numbers to quantify. Making comparisons between measurements provides an opportunity to connect number order with number magnitude in a concrete manner. Measuring offers a natural exposure to fractions, and contributes to one's conceptualization of more/less, taller/shorter, heavier/lighter, bigger/smaller, and near/far.

Some students have considerable difficulty picturing or incorporating the "feel" of distances and time spans. It is important for these students to measure items with which they are in daily contact in order to reinforce specific connections. For most children, it is helpful to gauge measurements in terms of self, so that a child may know that the family dog weighs half as much as the child, that the child's hand is big enough to hold two Ping Pong balls, that 20 of the child's footsteps equals the distance across the living room. Depending upon the particular learning difficulty of a given child, this may or may not be a useful paradigm for the unconventional student. Children who are inflexible and rigid in their thinking are unlikely to take into account their own growth and size changes. I hear echoes of children saying to me with great frustration, "But you told me that four of my hands is the same height as one of Daddy's feet!" or, "You said riding my bike around the block took up five minutes." These statements were probably made to the child at four or five years. The youngster is now 9 or 10 years old, but is still holding on to the outdated information. In such cases, it is better to give the child examples of states or measurements which are constant. For instance, a child could know that many men are about six feet tall. The child's forming a visual picture of a man equalling six feet can become a relatively reliable standard of measurement. In figuring out how high a flag pole is, the child might visualize four men standing on each other's shoulders. It might be helpful for a child to know how many inches around is a standard basketball or tennis ball. Children could measure their beds, their shoes, or their backyards to use as visual pictures of comparison. Recently, in buying a new front door, I was told that most doors are 36 inches by 80 inches, a fact of which I had absolutely no idea prior to the door-buying experience. It occurred to me that it would be helpful for children to know how long, tall, wide, and big around everyday things are. Measuring and estimating certainly go hand-in-hand in these kinds of game-exercises. Concepts of twice as big as, half as long as, and other part/whole relationships emerge naturally within this experimentation and discovery learning.

A poor sense of time and direction is often associated with mathematical weaknesses. Children with these difficulties become lost easily, and cannot find their way to a friend's house or to and from school. It is in this manner that their lives become restricted: they will not walk or ride to a friend's house because they are afraid they will not find the house; they are told to be home at four o'clock, but they cannot judge time or tell time, so they do not go, fearing that they will arrive at the wrong time. These students cannot judge the time needed to complete an assignment, to work on a project, or to go from here to there.

The importance of games in math learning cannot be overestimated. Many board games involve the use of numbers, sequencing, money, probability, and attention to detail. Cause and consequence are often critical elements of such games. Kamii's excellent book, *Young Children Reinvent Arithmetic* (1985), provides dozens of adaptations of store-bought games to teaching and learning mathematics and numeracy. Flexible parents and teachers will soon discover their own means of making adaptations to teach or to reinforce specific weaknesses. As illustrated by Kamii, children usually make their own modifications according to their needs and abilities. The observant teacher will recognize which students gravitate to or away from certain games, which is a clue to a child's strengths and weaknesses. Children who have trouble with spelling do not choose to play Scrabble or Boggle, while youngsters with math strengths often ask to play number, money, or dice games (Dominoes, Eights, Pay Day®, Monopoly®, Roll 'em, Twenty-Four). New math concepts are more easily assimilated when presented in game form, especially for children who perceive themselves to be troubled by numbers. Children like games which they can "pull" on their parents or other adults, and games with an element of chance are always appreciated because even the weaker students have some possibility of winning. In flash card contests, the less capable memorizer always loses; but games involving chance can help to even the score.

Graphing is another fundamental concept which needs to be incorporated into a child's mathematical studies. The collecting, organizing, and analyzing of data are problem-solving skills which permeate our lives. To be numerate, students must be able to read and make sense of graphic information, and they must understand the meaning of statistical terms such as average, mean, median, and mode. These terms emerge in all aspects of life, from grocery shopping to sports, from work to play, from house-buying to entertaining. Science, industry, medicine, education, business, and athletics all employ statistical analyses and graphs in their research, sales, teaching, and promotion.

Identifying what data to collect, and how to gather and record them, is the first step in the problem-solving process. The organizing, recording, and analyzing of the data are intimately relevant to problem-solving skills throughout one's life; and once again, depend upon development of metacognitive awareness and input. These processes give children first hand experience with numbers, classification, categorization, and with forming hypotheses and drawing conclusions. The analyzing of the data is critically pertinent to many problem-solving situations throughout one's life. This is an aspect of graphics which needs to be stressed, practiced, rehearsed, and emphasized for all students, but particularly so for those with learning delays. It is in the realm of analysis that learning disabled students often look weakest. Many, many trials, examples, and practices with various materials and in numerous situations should be presented so that students with cognitive delays and learning deficits can begin to draw meaningful conclusions and make appropriate generalizations.

The student experiencing difficulty with numbers needs carefully structured and well-planned instruction in mathematics as well as in everything else. Task analysis, setting specific objectives, and sequence planning are important processes to identify and work on. Allowance for sufficient time to learn and to assimilate each step of the process is mandatory.

SPECIFIC EXAMPLES OF TEACHING STRATEGIES

In *Succeed with Math* (1989), Tobias advocates looking at math competence as a way of problem solving rather than of getting correct answers. She states that she would prefer to grade students on their ability to approach a problem to be solved, on how many different ways they can solve it, and on how thoughtful an essay they can write about what makes a particular problem mathematically interesting. Furthermore, she observes that successful math students are those who understand their own style of thinking and those who actively engage in a process of problem solving. As suggested by Tobias, it may be extremely useful for students to hear from math experts about how they approach and cope with problems; about what they do when they forget what to do; about what they learn in the course of the struggle.

As is true in many other areas of learning, strategies for teaching children with numeracy deficits should be geared toward drawing upon the child's particular strengths and abilities. It is important to find out what does make sense to the child and to generalize that understanding to other problem situations. Teachers will usually find that instructions need to be modified and that expectations need to be adjusted according to the specific difficulties the student encounters.

Children with good memory abilities, for example, may do well to memorize math facts because it is actually quicker to "know" these facts; but children with very poor memory skills will spend their time more effectively by becoming proficient on calculators rather than on searching their memory bank for each fact. Both groups of children need to understand why and when one should perform a particular mathematical process. They need to understand that it is quicker to multiply than to add a series of the same numbers, and that one can sometimes divide rather than subtract.

Cooperative learning and small groups which are designed to problem solve together and out loud are effective "teachers" for children with number concept difficulties. Listening to another child's approach to a problem and observing a peer's method of dealing with mathematical situations can be tremendously instructive.

A child with visual-spatial dysfunctions can be a very misleading math student because the child may conceptually grasp the idea, but will tend to mix up the numbers or place them in the wrong columns or spaces so that the answer is often incorrect—even though the process and the understanding are well established. These students may perform more successfully with concrete materials and with oral examinations. Listening to this child talk about the problem and the child's approach to the problem may reveal a very different understanding from that which the student presented on paper. Students with visual-spatial involvements must be encouraged to use large-square graph paper, different colors to represent place value or columns, boxes around their final answers, limited numbers of problems per page, and good erasers. Concrete materials which represent numbers (Cuisenaire Rods, Dienes blocks, fraction bars) are extremely helpful for this group of students. A child with visual-spatial weaknesses may be rather poor at estimating sets, groups, distances, quantities, or amounts because the child has trouble with visualizing in general. On the other hand, this student may be good at estimating time, value, or other abstract concepts which are not visually based.

Children who have trouble with temporal or sequential organization have a different kind of mathematical profile. Understanding the concepts of time and money tend to be extremely difficult for them. They do not do well with multistep directions, and they frequently approach tasks in the wrong order. They usually copy slowly, which is similar to the visual-spatially impaired child, and one is likely to observe many mistakes in copied material.

The group of students which is weak sequentially and organizationally needs to be remediated by helping them to automatize number sequences and math facts. Rote activities which emphasize memory are helpful. The use of a calendar is mandatory because calendars offer predictable sequences of days, months, numbers, and seasons. Games and singing which involve rhymes for sequences and numbers are sometimes more easily learned than is material learned orally or from flash cards. Continuous reviews of sequential material (number counting, order, directions) will promote automaticity. Seriation of objects according to size, volume, weight, or position can be helpful for improving sequencing skills. As the children progress through elementary school, it will be important to initiate the teaching of practical life-skills, such as keeping a checkbook, balancing an account, handling money and making change, using calculators for everyday problems such as grocery shopping, ordering at restaurants, tipping, and going to the laundromat. Math examples which stress temporal sequences such as days of the week, time of day, schedules, routines, and algorithms are useful for enhancing sequencing skills.

Children with expressive and receptive language delays usually prefer nonverbal activities, and are sometimes quite a bit more proficient in math and science than they are in language arts or history. It is important to write directions for these students as they do not process them easily if given orally. Emphasis on paper-and-pencil tasks reduces anxiety for students with language deficits, and tends to produce more successful results. When taught with manipulatives, written instructions, and problems or equations given in small, component parts, math does not usually present as much of a problem to this group of children unless, of course, other learning dysfunctions are involved as well. Math worksheets which contain a model problem and a checklist of steps to follow are particularly good aids for language-delayed children. Learning the vocabulary of math will augment a child's math skills and enhance the development of language. Talking about a problem-solving process should be encouraged.

Following are examples of several math lessons which are good for all young children, but which have particular relevance to children with learning difficulties. This latter group of youngsters is likely to require more explanation, more discovery time, and more repetition of these lessons than will their peers, and they will need more direct teaching in generalizing what they have learned to other situations. Children with learning dysfunctions tend to acquire the specific material presented without being able to understand how it applies to similar experiences or problem-solving settings. For instance, learning how to find the perimeter of one's body may not generalize to finding the perimeter of one's backyard. While other students make these associations with maturity and development, the learning-delayed student usually does not; this child needs to be told that finding the area of the football field requires the same process as finding the area of the swimming pool, which is the same as finding the area of the cafeteria, and so on. Once again, what "makes sense" to other youngsters, what is learned by "osmosis," just does not seem to be available to students for whom learning is a problem. Patience and practice and the willingness to repeat concepts and processes will serve teachers and parents well.

1. The topic is PACES. Socks, color tiles in a cup or bag, construction paper, and pencils are required. The lesson reinforces counting skills and grouping by 10 while exposing students to the concept of perimeter and non-standard units of measure.

Step 1: Students will take a walk around the school or a playing field dropping a color tile into their sock every time they count 10 paces. Paces can be normal walking steps or toe-to-heel steps. An estimation component can be added here: before going outside, children may be asked to estimate the number of tiles they will need if one tile is dropped into the sock for every 10 paces. These tiles can be carried in a separate cup or bag.

Step 2: Back in the room, children count their color tiles saying 10, 20, 30, and so on. Children trace their footprint on a sheet of construction paper and cut it out. Children then record their total number of steps on their construction-paper footprint.

Discussion: The teacher introduces the word perimeter. "When you walk or measure around the outside of something, we call the distance around the outside the perimeter. The perimeter is similar to a fence around the outer edge."

Data Collection: "When I call on you, tell me how many paces it took for you to walk around the perimeter of the playground."

The teacher records each child's name and the number of paces on the chalkboard. The teacher then asks, "Why did it take Jake more steps than it took Lisa to walk around the perimeter of the playground?" This leading question should bring out the idea that the units of measurement, the paces, were not uniform.

The physical involvement and the active participation in this lesson make for a particularly good learning environment. Many different styles can be accommodated. Some children in the class may not be ready to count by 10s. The teacher could offer a choice so that a child could decide whether to count by 1s, 2s, 5s, or 10s. If a child does not understand the process of counting off and dropping the tiles in the sock, partners could be arranged so that one child would count, telling the other one when to drop the tile in the sock; or both could count, but one would tell the other when to put the tile in. A child in a wheelchair might be able to mark and count the revolutions of the wheel. Some children may want to put a tile in the sock every time they step on their right foot, which another student may say is the same as counting by 2s.

In the data collection, a child may say, "I have 50 tiles." Class members may want to help in figuring out whether this child counted by 10s or by some other number. Some children will not understand why the total number is not the same for everyone. If they have 30 tiles, they will think that everyone should have 30 tiles, or that 35 tiles is the "wrong answer." These are the students who have been exposed to a new concept, but have not yet mastered it. Teachers need to remember that all children will not master the same things in the same lesson, and that it is exposure and experience with the tasks which are the goals.

2. This lesson is called "Guess My Number" and is designed to practice place value and logical reasoning. No materials are required. Approximately 15 minutes will be needed initially to learn and to play the game. Subsequently, it can be used as a short filler, and it can serve as a teacher's quick assessment of a student's understanding of rounding and of place value.

Step 1: The teacher thinks of a two-digit number (e.g., 37) and tells the class: "My number rounded to the nearest ten is 40. Can you guess my number?"

Step 2: Students are called on to guess the number. In the above example, if a student guessed 43, the teacher would respond by saying, "You are right that 43 rounded to the nearest ten is 40, but that was not the number I was thinking of." If a student guessed 32, the teacher would respond that 32 rounded to the nearest ten would be 30, and thus could not be the number the teacher had in mind.

In this game, it would be helpful to write the clues on the chalkboard. The teacher would write: _____?_____ rounded to the nearest ten is 40. The teacher might want to write each student's guess as well, putting the possibilities in one column and the impossibilities in another.

Some students will benefit from having a number line on their desk in front of them while working out their guesses. While many children may be able to do their thinking in their heads, others will do better using pencil and paper.

Once again, partners or teams will be useful for some students. Discussing possible answers and weeding out impossible answers can be done cooperatively.

This game is a wonderful diagnostic tool for the observant teacher, who will want to be thinking about the kinds of errant guesses a child makes. If a child tries the number 32 on the first guess, the teacher may not know if this is a "wild" guess or if the child is actually "close." It may be a good idea to say: "Travis, I am going to give you three guesses. Thirty-two was not quite right, so why don't you try another number." If the child guesses 7, and follows that with 21, it could give the teacher different information than if the child suggests 45 and 36. Guesses of 45 and 36 may be random too, but perhaps not. The teacher will want to make a mental note or a note in a record book that Travis might be having trouble with rounding. It will be worth following up.

Although one needs to understand the process of rounding and of place value in order to make consistently good guesses, there is an element of chance, too, because anyone could guess the right answer at any time with absolutely no understanding of the process involved. It is this quirk which makes the game fun and which allows everyone to feel engaged in playing.

> Yogi Berra knew how to play the game: a waitress serving pizza asked him if he wanted his pizza cut into four pieces or into eight. "Better make it four," he replied. "I don't think I can eat eight."

(See appendix C for math idea and resource books, and for children's literature which pertains to mathematics and numeracy.)

SUMMARY: RECOGNIZING AND ATTENDING TO MATHEMATICAL DYSFUNCTIONS

POSSIBLE INDICATIONS OF NUMERACY DEFICITS

- children who have not developed the sense of one-to-one correspondence

- children who have difficulty with time, money, size, distance, order, seriation

- children who have trouble with concepts of more/less, before/after, up/down

- children for whom dates, calendars, schedules seem to have little meaning

- students who do not understand or have a sense of numerical relationships, patterns, probability, chance

- students who do not appreciate the idea of estimating or who do not understand the concept of statistics

- students who have demonstrated specific memory or sequencing difficulties in other areas as well as in math

- children with fine motor difficulties, or with organizational weaknesses, or with visual perceptual deficits—these children make computational errors, but they comprehend mathematical concepts

WHAT TO DO

Memory deficits: teach process, and allow students to use number lines, calculators, numerical tables, charts, and so on for computational purposes.

Sequencing difficulties: practice seriation with many different kinds of manipulatives; use calendars and rulers; post number lines, tables, charts, math facts on student's desk; help student to be orderly. Emphasize doing tasks in a step-by-step process. Review what happens first; then what happens next, and so on. Many of these children can and should learn to memorize, make automatic, a number of math facts and formulas. Memorizing does not take the place of comprehension, but of sequencing and of ordering.

Fine motor and/or visual motor weaknesses: use graph paper, wide-ruled paper, few problems per page; do *not* have child copy from the chalkboard or from a book; monitor to see that problems are lined up and written correctly, and check to see that there are no number reversals. Allow many opportunities for oral work. Test orally if there are many written errors.

Language delays: use a partner or cooperative learning when doing word problems and in order to verify directions; present materials in both written and spoken formats; offer many different kinds of examples, and give a sample problem and solution to which the student has ready access.

Number concept weaknesses: use literature at the appropriate developmental level; constantly make associations to real-life situations; give many practical examples; show where and why various numbers or number relationships are used; play games which involve time, money, numbers. Talk about size, distance, patterns, measurements in day-to-day situations. Compare and contrast.

Poor problem-solving approaches or inflexible strategizing: model, talk about, and use various problem-solving strategies. Compare several strategies and let the student evaluate which ones are best, and tell why. Present situations which have no correct answer, and problems which can be solved in more than one way.

IN GENERAL

Manipulatives are probably more critical in math than in any other subject. Use them for size, weight, number, measuring, seriation, grouping, comparing, estimating, and graphing.

Offer practical applications for everything which is taught in math. Show students why they might want to know about adding or subtracting, fractions, distance, counting, and estimating.

For children who do *not* have memory dysfunctions, it is easier and faster to memorize math facts than it is to figure them out or to use a calculator. (Children with good memories should not become overreliant on clever strategizing because it is always faster to "know" something than it is to figure it out.) Children who *do* have memory difficulties should be given tools (software, calculators, manipulatives, mnemonic devices) to facilitate the computing of answers.

Developing compensatory skills and learning alternative problem-solving strategies are important components in math. Sometimes skills need to be strengthened and sometimes they need to be circumvented if there are other viable means of accomplishing the task.

REFERENCE LIST

Holt, John. (1989) *Learning All the Time.* New York: Addison-Wesley Publishing.

Hutchins, Pat. (1987) *Changes, Changes.* New York: Macmillan.

Johnson-Martin, Nancy, Susan Attermeier, and Bonnie Hacker. (1990) *The Carolina Curriculum for PreSchoolers with Special Needs*. Baltimore: Paul Brookes Publishing Co.

Kamii, Constance. (1985) *Young Children Reinvent Arithmetic*. New York and London: Teachers College Press.

Morel, Eve, ed. (1973) *Goldilocks*. In *Fairy Tales and Fables*. New York: Grosset & Dunlop.

Paulos, John Allen. (1988) *Innumeracy*. New York: Hill and Wang.

Ritchhart, Ronald. (1991) Exploring Our Numeracy: Moving beyond Number Sense. Master's Thesis, University of Colorado; Addison and Wesley, forthcoming.

Sharmat, Marjorie. (1978) *Big Fat Enormous Lie*. New York: Dutton.

Tobias, Sheila. (1987) *Succeed with Math*. New York: College Board Publications.

7

Parents and Teachers Together

Parents are people, people with children....
— Marlo Thomas

Who you are is more important than what you teach.
— Unknown

I know that there is something the matter with my child ... but maybe the problem is not with Allan. Maybe I'm the problem. Should I tell the teacher that I think Allan is different from other kids? Will that prejudice the teacher against him? against me? If I wait-and-see, is it going to be better or worse ...?

THE UNCERTAINTY OF LEARNING DIFFICULTIES

Most parents of unconventional children face this dilemma when their child begins preschool, and then re-face it each year as school begins again. One is never quite sure if alerting a teacher to a child's differences is going to improve the situation or detract from it. The adults involved are ambivalent, and research into learning difficulties and the school provides no definitive answer because, ultimately, it always comes down to the individual child, teacher, and parent. This is particularly true in the early grades. An eighth grader who reads at a fourth-grade level and who cannot divide is obviously experiencing some learning dysfunctions. However, a second grader who has not emerged as a reader and is having trouble with adding is not remarkably different from many other second-grade children. One is not sure if that child is a late bloomer, has learning disabilities, or if emotional difficulties are interfering with learning.

Similarly, some teachers jump on the bandwagon, immediately identifying a child who learns differently; while other teachers never refer a child for an evaluation or consultation. Parents manifest the same incongruities, with some families wanting their child "labeled" in order to have special services provided; while other families adamantly insist that their unconventional youngster be treated "the same as everyone else." Many pediatricians tell parents that their child is very likely to grow out of whatever the stage may be, but others advocate intervention and remediation so as not to impede further the developmental delay.

Uncertainty pervades! If a child has a broken leg, no one questions the cast, the need for excused gym, the caregiving supplements, and the additional emotional support required. It is relatively certain that within a few weeks, the child will have outgrown the stage. On the other hand, the hidden handicaps of learning and living difficulties are characterized by ambiguity and unpredictability. No one knows for sure what might happen next. Understandably, teachers and parents feel inadequately trained and prepared for working with unconventional children. While everyone acknowledges the importance of the parent-teacher relationship, little is done to prepare either party for this involvement.

Though well intentioned, many teachers are anxious about the child who is learning differently. Teachers have a general expectation that all students in their classroom will be pretty much the same; otherwise, they probably do not belong there. Teachers may not know how to plan for children who do not fit the mold, so they become scared and resentful of these students and their parents. Teachers may sense that they will not be able to provide the child with an appropriate learning environment, that their teaching may be criticized, and that they will be accountable for a child whom they could not serve. Thus, teachers confront themselves on a daily basis with their own perceived failure. A teacher who is in this situation is likely to begin to blame the child for not learning; but, sometimes, even very willing children cannot manage their own behaviors or learning abilities well enough to meet the guidelines for success.

Interestingly, parents worry about these classroom issues in much the same way that teachers do; on top of which, they continuously are anxious about their own parental inadequacies. Parents wonder if their children will be properly educated, if they will be criticized as parents, and if their child who is different will be "kicked out" of school. They want to know how the school can help and how they can be effective partners; yet, all too often, the cooperative effort between parents and teachers is invalidated by mutual fear and resentment. The fact that teachers have had parents and parents have had teachers leads to both positive and negative carry-over attitudes. Furthermore, some teachers *are* parents, just as some parents *are* teachers. Nevertheless, it is infrequently the case that these common denominators, which could foster compassion and empathy, are played out positively.

One skilled kindergarten teacher, who is not a parent, said, "Awareness and empathy come from knowing children in their own homes. I always make home visits." An aspect of home visits which appeals to this teacher is that going to the child's house offers the child a "one-up-manship in that it is the child's turf, not mine."

Almy (1975) points out that not all of those who choose to work with young children are equally as enthusiastic about or adept at working with adults. The role of the early childhood educator calls for a considerable amount of contact with adults as well as with children, but this is an aspect of teaching which may be overlooked when one chooses one's profession. Teacher education programs would do well to require more direct instruction in and practical experience with parent-teacher relationships. Although the teacher should not be placed in the role of counselor or therapist, it would be beneficial to provide classes for teachers in communication skills. Similarly, teachers could feel more comfortable with unconventional students and their parents, as well as with themselves, if they were given more specific instruction in the needs and difficulties experienced by children with various learning styles. Moreover, it would be helpful if teachers could be understanding about the responsibilities carried by a parent of an involved child. At the same time, they need to guard against assuming that there are problems when none exist. (In some countries, would-be teachers are required to spend some time living with another family in order to gain a sense of the demands of the parental roles.)

While it is fair to say that the teacher knows better than anyone else what the child is like in the classroom, it must be acknowledged equally that parents are the experts concerning what the child is like at home. Without this respect for and recognition of expertise, parents and teachers will have trouble seeing the same child. One first-grade teacher stated emphatically, if somewhat metaphorically, "I kept telling the parents that the Emperor was wearing no clothes, but they refused to see it!"

> Keith is six years old, an only child in a very quiet home with parents who spend much time reading and painting. His parents, who are in their late forties, have offices at home. Keith considers his room to be his office and enjoys spending time alone, quietly, in this space. Like his parents, he reads, draws, and builds happily for hours on his own.

Having had numerous ear infections in his first few years, Keith is overly sensitive to loud noise, and he experiences some auditory confusion when there is a lot of stimulation in his environment.

Keith attends an "open school" in which there are no walls separating the pod-classrooms. He has not adjusted well to first grade, making few friends and behaving aggressively in class. His teacher says that he is always out of his seat, wandering around, and not participating in group activities. She remarks to Keith's parents that he "probably has an attention deficit" and that "he needs to be in a special class for children who have behavioral difficulties."

Keith's parents think the teacher must have their child mixed up with someone else's. This is not at all the little boy they know at home.

Where unconventional children are concerned, teachers are always feeling on the edge, wondering if they are doing the right thing. Intense as this feeling is, it probably pales in comparison to the way parents feel. As recognized by Silver in *The Misunderstood Child* (1984), the child with learning difficulties has more than educational problems because the same difficulties which interfere with academics are likely to interfere with the child's social and emotional development as well. Parents are usually aware of these difficulties long before school. Young ones with developmental vulnerabilities are often those who do not bond easily as infants. Important developmental issues of trust, confidence, predictability, separation, and individuation can be delayed or interfered with as a result of the child's poor adaptability to the environment. Interpersonal relationships suffer, with parents and siblings becoming affected by the unconventional child in the family.

In *The Difficult Child* (1985), Turecki discusses family interaction, pointing out that a child's innate temperament is not "the fault" of the parents or of anyone else, but it does make family members and other caretakers angry, and it does make such children hard to raise. He emphasizes that the results of parental handling depend not only on what parents do, but also on what the child brings to the situation. Parents and teachers, therefore, will want to replace confrontation with concrete management techniques which are compatible with the child's temperament and abilities.

In a poignant article concerning the nation's care of its children, Lance Morrow (*Time* 1990, p. 78), wrote:

> Home is all the civilization that a child knows. Home is one of nature's primal forms, and if it does not take shape properly around the child, then his mind will be at least a little homeless all its life.

Although it is true that children who come from disadvantaged home lives are at risk for learning difficulties (Pediatric Round Table Discussions 1983), many youngsters exhibiting learning deficits live in very attentive, productive, well-educated, functional families. Moreover, all parents want what is best for their children. It is knowing what might be best, or how to acquire it, which usually precipitates the confrontations between families and schools. An objective, problem-solving approach can be effective in resolving these differences.

> Mr. Richards is a first-grade teacher who has been perplexed for several months by David's volatile outbursts in the classroom. Frequently well behaved and relatively docile, David periodically explodes, turning frantically disruptive, grabbing pencils, paper, and books from other children, storming out of the room, screaming loudly in the halls. This behavior seems to be unprovoked by anything Mr. Richards has been able to observe or identify. It is not unusual for David to fall asleep after he has behaved in this manner.
>
> Not being able to put his finger on anything specific, Mr. Richards has been reluctant to mention it to David's parents. For the most part, David is an average student, although he sometimes has trouble making conceptual connections, and he sometimes appears to be daydreaming during class.
>
> At home, Mrs. Archer is relieved to have David in school a full day, and she hopes that he has not exhibited any of his outrageous tantrums. Since she has heard nothing from the school, she assumes that David is doing fine. On the other hand, she is growing increasingly anxious about her own parenting skills, wondering why David behaves so erratically and temperamentally with her if he does not act this way at school. It concerns her that David's father spanks him for this behavior, but she is afraid that she might be too docile in her handling of David.
>
> In November, school-parent conferences are arranged. Mr. Richards has rehearsed 80 ways of approaching David's parents about their son's behavior. His worst fears are realized as the

Archers enter the room looking defensive and anxious. Rather than beating around the bush, Mr. Richards has decided to take a direct tack: "In addition to all of the good things I can and want to tell you about David, I need to tell you, too, that I am confused by one aspect of David's behavior ... "

As he describes David's outbursts, Mrs. Archer begins to cry, but interrupts to say, "I thought he only did that with me."

A warm and informative conversation follows. Mr. Richards asks for some help, "Have you found an effective way to handle this behavior at home? What would you like for me to do about it?"

Since no one has found a viable means of dealing with these "tantrums," Mr. Richards suggests that they consult with the school psychologist and the school nurse. The nurse informs them that David's behavior is not dissimilar from some children who have seizures. A medical evaluation is recommended. Ultimately, the results of an EEG do confirm psychomotor seizures. David is put on medication.

Mr. Archer is astounded, but somewhat relieved. Mr. Richards and Mrs. Archer feel better about their teacher/parent management abilities. Everyone feels more at ease, including David, whose relationship with others improves rather dramatically.

It goes without saying that this encounter could have been handled in many different ways, some of which would have increased everyone's anxiety and tension. When both parties make a concerted effort to describe behavior rather than to be judgmental of it, the conversation usually is smoother. Some good phrases for teachers to keep in mind fall into the category of "I messages" advocated by Gordon (1975) and Ginott (1971). It is also helpful to ask questions of parents in order to understand the child being discussed:

"I am confused by ... "

"I was wondering about ... "

"I think that I need you to tell me more about your child."

"What do you find works best with your child?"

"This is what I am seeing at school. Does your child do this at home, too?"

Sometimes the family does not recognize the same behaviors as those that the teacher describes (refer back to the story about Keith, whose teacher and parents observed two entirely different children), and sometimes the parents are not willing to be engaged in the process of dealing with the problem since they feel it is up to the school to handle it. If the teacher has described objective observations, there is no need to prove either the teacher or the parents right or wrong. The teacher is in a position to say: "This is what happens at school. Do you have some thoughts about how you would like me to handle your child?" or, "This is how I am thinking I would like to deal with these issues. How do you feel about my taking this approach?"

When there is no judgment about the character of the child, the parent, or the teacher, and when the behavior or learning difficulty is framed in terms of an objective problem which needs to be solved, there is opportunity for joint effort and mutual cooperation. One might just as easily be saying, "There is not enough fresh air in this classroom. What can we do about that?" as saying, "Bonnie is writing many of her letters and numbers backward. How can we think of ways to change that?"

Parents have a legitimate expectation that school is a place where children go to learn. If the child is not learning, there is the concomitant assumption that the school is not doing its job, and it is around the non-learning child that schools and parents fall into combat. In all fairness to parents, teachers also have a tendency to suggest that there is something incompetent about the home life of those students who are not measuring up in class. Teachers will want to focus on making statements that do not make parents feel defensive about themselves or their children. "I am finding it hard to help Nadine learn how to read" is more comfortable than "Your child isn't learning how to read." "It concerns me that Ryan seems to need to get out of his seat so often" is softer than "Ryan won't stay at his desk and do his work." "Do you have some ideas about what to do when Larry forgets to bring his things to school?" engages the parents in the process of making a change. If the parents throw it back on the teacher, saying that the teacher should be able to figure out how to handle the class and that they have enough to do at home, the teacher can respond by sharing with the parents how the teacher has chosen to handle the difficulty, and asking the parents for their affirmation of that approach: "Is it all right with you if I have Larry stay after school for 15 minutes on Wednesdays to complete his assignments?"

As with all of the teaching and learning strategies which have been discussed in this book, sensitivity, flexibility, and an awareness of individual style and personality must dominate the tactic chosen. In truth, both teachers and parents want to be friendly and want to help children. Respect, the Golden Rule, and honesty with kindness serve one well. Plain old-fashioned talking, sharing, and feeling seem to work best. Skillful communication takes practice and experience, coupled with genuine caring and understanding. Teachers and parents need to try hard because difficult news is not easy to relate or to hear. Schools might consider using trained facilitators to help negotiate some of the more troublesome conferences and staffings. A professional mediator would be invaluable for teaching communication skills at faculty in-service meetings as well.

REFERENCE LIST

Almy, Millie. (1975) *The Early Childhood Educator at Work*. New York: McGraw-Hill.

Brown, Catherine Caldwell, ed. (1983) Childhood Learning Disabilities and Prenatal Risk. Paper presented at Johnson & Johnson Baby Products' Pediatric Round Table Discussion, Skillman, NJ.

Comfort, Randy Lee. (1981) *The Unconventional Child*. Denver, CO: Randy Lee Comfort.

Ginott, Haim G. (1971) *Between Parent and Child*. New York: Avon Books.

Gordon, Thomas. (1975) *Parent Effectiveness Training*. New York: New American Library.

Morrow, Lance. (1990) "The Bright Cave under the Hat." *Time* 136, no. 27: 78.

Silver, Larry. (1984) *The Misunderstood Child*. New York: McGraw-Hill.

Turecki, Stanley, and Leslie Tonner. (1985) *The Difficult Child*. New York: Bantam Books.

8

General Accommodations and Adaptations for Classroom Teachers

Progress always involves risk. You can't steal second base and keep your foot on first.
—Frederick Wilcox

Limply folded into the narrow wheelchair, Harriet balanced the tea cup with the back of her right hand and the left side of her nose—a rather unusual strategy for tea-drinking. The logistics defied physics, but accomplished the task, and personified the indomitable spirit of an 81-year-old woman whose life had been spent accommodating and adapting her situation to her environment.

When I met Harriet, I was so magnetized by her that I knew she would soon become a special friend. My fleeting observations of her across the dining room, however, had not taken into account how enormously difficult it would be to maintain my own strength for our relationship. At 81, she reflected a life, a history, a grace of time already passed. From birth, she had been disenfranchised by cerebral palsy, but there had been a time when she could walk with supports and when she could talk somewhat more accessibly. She was well educated and well informed, and she was endowed with a superb memory. I discovered all of this through the disjointed antics of communication which her insatiable perseverance and my acquired patience enabled us to share. Understanding Harriet's verbal conversation was an exhausting, frustrating, confusing, but always gratifying task for us both.

Eventually, I made her a book in which she pointed to pictures expressing her basic needs and thoughts: "I am hungry," "I need to go to the bathroom," "I want pen and paper," and so forth. I bought her reams of paper and many pens. She loved different-colored pens. I wrote in Harriet's daily diary for her, and I allowed her to eat by herself, which she wanted to do, instead of feeding her myself, which would have been faster. I never did, and probably never will, stop thinking about the many strategies which could ease and make lighter Harriet's daily struggles.

Despite the fact that my usual work is with children, I learned from this lovely, older woman much that can be shared with and applied to the lives of many younger people. Like the children who come to see me, Harriet altruistically offered an openness and a willingness which enabled me to learn as much or more than I am ever able to teach. Harriet's tenacious persistence confirmed for me the uniqueness of individual personality and the power of relentless desire. Even when I grew tired and frustrated, she would not let go. It was she who gave me continued courage, and it is because of her that I am inspired to keep searching for ways to defy difference.

In this final chapter, which is concerned with accommodations and adaptations that teachers can use in their own classrooms, I hope to emphasize that there is no one way of doing things, no one right answer. At the risk of being redundant, it is important to stress that teaching all children, not just unconventional children, needs to be a creative, reciprocal, flexible process. Knowing that a child is stronger visually than auditorily gives the parent and teacher a clue about where to begin with the child; it does not determine a recipe-written program of teaching. The often asked question, "What are you going to do about this child with learning disabilities?" should not have a pat answer. The response needs to be framed in terms of learning with the student about the ways in which that particular student acquires information most effectively, how the student can be most productive, and what makes learning appealing or interesting for that student. It is a trial-and-error process, but the "trials" are not random. The teacher must decide why a particular approach is being instituted and what kinds of results could be expected in a given amount of time.

ADAPTING CLASSROOMS TO MEET INDIVIDUAL NEEDS

This chapter deals with strategies for adapting your classroom to meet individual needs. It presents strategic ideas and various possibilities of how and why a teacher may begin making accommodations in the classroom. If these suggestions do not work, don't give up! Try something else; talk to another colleague who might have yet another approach; ask the student to tell you more about the way learning makes sense; invite the parents to let you in on what has been successful for them. Strategies are not answers; they are a means of discovering and investigating rather than a mandate of absolute rules. There is a lot of mistake-making, re-adjusting, re-creating, and trying again which happens in the process of figuring out what will work.

Adjusting to differences becomes the challenge for teachers who must meet the needs of the 20 to 30 youngsters who make up their classrooms each day. As more and more children with learning and living differences become integrated into regular classes, the population of students becomes increasingly diverse—but not more diverse, actually, than the teachers who teach, the families who parent, the children who gather together on the street corner. With diversity in mind, Bailey (1990) has advocated "normalization" of classrooms, a concept which incorporates more than what has been referred to in the past as mainstreaming. Normalization includes the use of the environment, the physical setting, the teaching strategies, the family involvement, and the social services which are integral to the school community. Furthermore, normalization is a concept which is directed toward making available to everyone within the educational facility patterns of life and of schooling which coincide with everyday living and regular life circumstances.

Clark (1986) and Galinsky and David (1988) substantiate the importance of the environmental milieu. Clark purports that "intellectual progress must be understood in terms of the brain interacting with the experiences of the environment to either strengthen or deny one's genetic endowment" (p. 8). "Intelligence," she continues, "may well rest on the effectiveness of opportunities and experiences provided by the child's home and school." Galinsky and David support this point of view, and suggest that learning is a problem-solving process which, when worked effectively, "promotes not only intellect, but also resilience and good mental health in one's daily life" (introduction).

When one considers the importance of the total learning environment, the value of an integrated educational approach becomes increasingly obvious because this manner of teaching allows students to work from their areas of strength and interest, and because it enables teachers to discover and to utilize each child's most effective mode of learning. An additional benefit is that the teaching process becomes more varied and more creative for the instructor as well as for the students. Usually, a teacher will have much to gain in reciprocal learning settings because children are full of surprises in what they know and do not know. Often, when I am caught off-guard by a child's ability to do something, I will ask: "How did you know that?" or "How did you learn that?" Here are some of the myriad wonderful responses that children have offered:

> I memorized it with rhymes.
>
> It's like a T.V. commercial I know.
>
> My brother showed me how to do it.
>
> My sister put it in a cheerleading routine for me.
>
> I tapped out a rhythm for it.
>
> My friend went to Arizona and brought back a snake just like that one.
>
> I drew a picture of it in my head.
>
> It's the same number of people in our family, and we have four girls and four boys.

Sometimes the example one child gives me works for another child, and sometimes it does not; but it is inevitably more thought-provoking than teaching the same thing in the same way all of the time.

When considering strategies, it is imperative that one adopt an attitude of flexibility. If a child has not been able to grasp a concept or to learn a skill within a usual amount of time, it is safe to assume that a new approach rather than more of the same is worth a try. Mae West once said, "In choosing between two evils, I always choose the one I haven't tried before." Essentially, the same probably holds true in teaching—if one method does not seem to be working, try another.

Diagnostic teaching involves insight into and understanding of the characteristics of a child's approach to problem solving. An appreciation of individual style always is helpful in determining the specific teaching strategies one designs. An approach that works for one student will not necessarily work equally for another student. A few discouraging stories will serve to illustrate this point.

> A fifth-grade special education teacher works with a child who had just come into my practice. I asked the teacher what she was doing to remediate the child's reading/writing difficulties. The teacher named a well-known phonetic language program. When I asked why she had chosen this program, the teacher responded that she feels it is a good program and one with which she has had a lot of success. I agree that it is a good phonetic method, and that *with the right child*, it can be a successful teaching tool; however, I would have preferred a response from the teacher which included an understanding of this particular child's needs and strengths in conjunction with the choosing of a program. As it turns out, this student is weak auditorily and strong visually. A phonetically based approach is likely to be infinitely more frustrating and debilitating than a visually based program would be. Recognition of sight words, memorizing commonly used words, and learning about family words would be more effective with this child—despite the fact that the teacher is using what is generally considered to be a very effective phonics format.
>
> The mother of a third-grade child I see in my practice called me about a rather unusual approach which the child's teacher was advocating. The boy has a fair amount of trouble with directionality, in that it is difficult for him to remember left and right, before and after, in front of, next to, and so on. He is somewhat ambidextrous, writing with his left hand, but doing almost everything else with his right hand. The child is a very poor speller, and reads below age level. His teacher, "in an effort to improve his spelling," is requiring that he learn to spell words forward and *backward*.

Being the practical person I am, I cannot begin to comprehend why one who has trouble learning the everyday, necessary, useful information about life and school would want to take on the enormously difficult, irrelevant task of spelling words backward. Unless one is into creating palindromes (Was it a rat I saw) or word configurations (mom/dad/wow), there is never a reason to spell a word backward! Doing so is the kind of antic children devise when they choose not to pay attention in class, or when they want to make up code languages.

It would be reasonable for a child to be taught to look at the first and last letters of a word to be sure that the child reads or spells the word from the beginning. A student with directional difficulties could be taught the fact that in the English language, all words are spelled from left to right, and all reading material begins on the left. I would put a sticker on a young child's left hand, put an arrow at the beginning (left side) of words and reading matter, concentrate on the fact that the writing hand for the above child is the left one. I might create a phrase such as "Look Left" for the child to refer to. In this case, there would not be much reason to talk about reading from left to right because if the child starts on the left, there is no place else to go but right. Color coding, green-for-go, for the first word or letter is helpful for young children.

Whenever one begins to work with a child, it is a good idea to ask oneself:

Why would I pick this method of instruction for this child?

What does the child need?

Can this strategy meet those needs?

How will I know if the needs are being met?

Recently, I evaluated a seventh grader who has been in a good specialized school for a few years and who will be returning now to public school. The boy's ability to decode sight words is very weak, but he reads in context fairly adequately and his comprehension and self-correcting skills are at or above grade level. The special education teacher would like to improve his decoding of sight words. In the early grades, I might agree with that approach; but in this case, I feel that it is important for a seventh grader to concentrate on contextual reading. There are relatively few times in the real world when we need to read sight words. A stop sign, street name, cereal label, and map directions come to mind as examples, but this particular child can do most of that, and most of these words are not as frequently encountered or needed as the day-to-day reading of schoolwork, newspapers, magazines, and books for enjoyment. For this child, educational strategies are best directed toward reading for meaning, toward developing study skills (highlighting, paraphrasing, outlining), and toward making sense of and being able to generalize the knowledge. It is my impression that a 14-year-old student will be further turned off of learning if the student has to spend time decoding lists of words; whereas learning how to do a research paper on the history of soccer might be more likely to engage him in the reading process.

Typically, the major concern teachers in mainstreamed classrooms express is how to accommodate for diverse levels of readiness and style. Adjustments can pertain more to method than to content. In all classrooms, different students will achieve at different rates and in different ways. If several people go together to a symphony concert, they will not all appreciate the music identically. The piano student might attend more carefully to the piano solo than to the orchestra; the woodwind afficionado may focus on the slightly off-tune oboe; the back specialist will note the conductor's poor spinal alignment; and the exhausted parent may take a bit of a nap and be delighted to have had a musical atmosphere in which to relax. After the concert, each of these people may express that it was a lovely outing. This kind of diverse interest and attentiveness occurs in every classroom every day. The teacher will not want to expect that all children ingest exactly the same information from a lesson. If the teacher's goal is that children become engaged in some meaningful way, at whatever level, then the teacher can reach many more students. A good goal is that each child learns or contributes something during most of the day's lessons.

"Thinking aloud" has become a good teaching strategy both educationally and psychologically. All problem solvers need to plan a strategy to get from the initial problem state to the desired goal. Throughout the day, many situations arise which are solved quite automatically, such as eating when hungry, sharpening a pencil when it breaks, or answering the phone when it rings. For school children with learning dysfunctions, however, many problems are not easily resolved. Asking a child to think out loud enables the child to focus attention on the specific end, and on the means of getting there, and it allows the instructor to gain insight into the child's thought process. Perhaps the student is able to identify the problem but cannot figure out any way to deal with the problem, or maybe the child can generate only one solution to solve it. (Are there other possible solutions which would be easier, faster, or more effective?)

Children with learning deficits, as has been mentioned earlier, tend to be constricted in their problem-solving abilities. They are usually not flexible in their selection of strategies and they are often not efficient in their problem-solving solutions. Many cannot monitor the effectiveness of their solutions.

A kindergarten child may walk outside and around half the school building to get to the gym because that is the only way the child was shown to get to a room that is actually directly across the hall from the kindergarten, if one goes out the other door.

A second grader wears the same shirt every day because someone once said that it was a nice shirt.

A fourth grader tells his mother that he hates lasagna, so mother fixes the same meal and tells the boy it is Italian pie, and he eats it right up.

There is very little risk-taking among youngsters with learning difficulties, partially because once the child has finally learned one way of doing something, it is too hard or too scary to try it a different way. The child will learn one way which is safe and then will stick to that method uncompromisingly—which is one reason why many children with learning dysfunctions also have social problems.

Earlier chapters have described some of the clues for identifying children who are learning and living differently. For instance, there was the suggestion that the young child who is unable to share, to be flexible, and to compromise often is demonstrating more than a personality trait. Children who cannot deal with schedule changes, who cannot switch partners, places, teams, or books, who cannot make a transition from one teacher to another or from one room to another, or those who cannot understand why they are always in trouble, may be experiencing a learning difficulty rather than reflecting a behavior problem. Teachers were asked to note the child who seemed to need to be taught many skills which most other children were learning by peer association. Teachers will want to keep a running record of incidents in which these children have trouble. This recordkeeping helps to identify patterns. Observing and describing this child more carefully might lead to assessment of and planning for the specific needs relevant to the child's growth and development.

When a teacher notices that a child is having trouble keeping up with the class, it is often a good idea for the teacher to take the child aside during a lunch or recess period to talk about what is happening. It could be helpful for the student and the teacher to have a private understanding of what is expected by the teacher, of what is going on for the child, of how certain standards can be met or complied with. For example, if the student does not understand the instructions, the teacher might advise the child that there will be a special time that the teacher will come around to the child's desk to go over the directions or to clarify the assignment so that the student does not need to keep asking questions or saying, "I don't understand." When children feel less singled out and when they are reassured that they will get the help that they need, they usually behave better and feel less anxious.

Teachers who remind their classes about schedules and transitions will find that they have less difficulty with moving from one thing to another. Writing the schedule on the chalkboard, and then reminding the class that "You have five more minutes before we clean up to go to music," or "Be sure to watch the clock while you are doing your art projects because we only have 20 minutes in which to complete this work," will help most of the students stay on task and move along in their work. There are always some, however, who keep irregular schedules. As the teacher walks around the room while children are working, the teacher could quietly remind the usual stragglers that they have only a few more minutes or that it is almost time to go to physical education. Giving these little time alerts and schedule warnings can be useful aids for children who move slowly or who are oblivious to time.

Charts tend to be good organizers, also. Most little children like to mark off what they have completed by making checks or sticking stickers onto a chart. On the other hand, child-attended charts take a good bit of teacher monitoring, and some teachers may find that this is too time-consuming. In discussing consistency with me, one teacher said, "Teachers have to give up a lot of their own time in order to mean-what-you-say!" That is very true, so it is especially important for teachers not to overload themselves because just the daily routine can seem pretty full in and of itself.

In order to combat teacher overload, and as a means of facilitating interpersonal relationships, particularly in the early grades, the partnership plan becomes an extremely useful teaching tool. Teachers can pair children up for various activities in different ways so that the same children are not always allowed to be "chosen" or "more popular." Sometimes the children might be able to select their own buddy, but more often the teacher should make assignments, being sure to talk about how partnerships work, how people need to learn to work together, and how each of us can be helpful to someone else in different ways. For the shy or withdrawn child, a special friend decreases loneliness and isolation. For the slower-learning child, a partner offers helpful instructions and leadership, reducing the teacher's need to give constant attention and time to each child who is having difficulty at school. One child may need only a reading partner; another child may do well in the classroom, but needs a buddy for lunch and recess. A child who needs help during math may be able to offer help during reading or physical education. Giving children special responsibilities which coincide with their strengths is very reinforcing and tends to reduce the demands made on the teacher. The teacher does not personally have to be 100 percent in charge of everything which is taught in the classroom, but the teacher is responsible for figuring out how to get the needs met. Students can be active participants in this process.

A cooperative learning model is dependent upon good teacher planning and input, but young children have a lot to learn from one another, and they believe in each other more than they believe in adults. Children are good observers of other children. They mimic what their peers do and say — some more advantageously or detrimentally than others. Peers also have an insightful sense of what is meaningful to another child.

> A second-grade teacher had trouble getting across to Neil the concept of one less. Brandon blurted out, "You know, Neil, like when you had to run twice in the relay because we had one less on our team." "Got it!" said Neil.

"Let me show you" is a commonly heard phrase among young children, but kids do not like it when teachers or parents say that to them. They only accept it from their friends. A teacher will benefit from asking Charlotte to show Valerie how to distribute the homework papers in the proper boxes because Valerie likes Charlotte and wants to do what she can do. Kevin, who constantly loses his belongings and his school papers, may become more attentive to organizing his affairs if bringing his homework to class earns him partner time with Scott, who is his very best friend.

Accommodating for unconventionality also is possible on specific assignments. If a page of arithmetic problems is handed out, a slow child might be asked to do only the right column, or the last line, or every other line. That child will feel successful by accomplishing what was individually assigned, even if it is not the entire page of problems. A child who has trouble writing may be asked to write a list of words which convey the important points in the story rather than writing complete sentences or a full paragraph. When a report is due, a child with multiple language-based difficulties may be told that the report will be graded for content, for ideas, but not for spelling or punctuation. Another time, this student can be given sentences to write which will be graded for spelling or punctuation, but not for content. Children who have trouble with spelling but who are not experiencing other language-based delays rarely write as competently or as innovatively as they speak because they are reluctant to use vocabulary which they know but cannot spell. From time to time, it is a good idea to let them write to express thoughts rather than limiting them by marking down for spelling.

Individualizing the goals and the tasks allows for all children to strive for a reachable accomplishment within the same lesson. Teachers do not have to make up 25 different lessons to match 25 different needs. One lesson with many different expectation levels can satisfy the whole class.

> The lesson is painting. One child will be happy to paint with red first, and then with orange; while another child will realize that mixing red and yellow makes orange. A third child will ask how to spell red and yellow. Somebody says, "Let's mix some more colors." What happens? "Let's mix all of the colors!"

> The lesson is hats. Terry has learned to spell "hat," and is happy making up sentences about people and animals wearing hats. Kelly figures out all of the words which rhyme with hat. Molly creates a poem using hat-family words. Jay is in the dress-up corner trying on many different hats, experimenting with the roles people play when wearing various hats. Tynan teaches the word "hat" in Vietnamese, and Antonio says it in Spanish. Everyone is learning.

Several modifications of reading/writing activities were detailed in chapter 5, and ideas for math lessons were described in chapter 6. There is no end to the possibilities of accommodations and extensions which can be available within any given lesson. Creativity, sometimes eccentricity, and flexibility are the keys. The teacher is the planner and the facilitator, and the teacher certainly must be well prepared; but the class is always available for teaching and learning together.

It has been suggested repeatedly throughout this book that no one is totally free of learning difficulties. For all of us, some material is harder to learn than is other material. Moreover, even when we have learned certain material, it may not feel as comfortable to us as does certain other knowledge. When I do assessments, I know that I have to be very careful in the presentation of the visual portions of evaluations because that is an area of weakness for me. I have done most of these many, many times; I know them well, but they are still harder for me than are other aspects of the procedures.

Some people are less aware of their own weaknesses because they do not manifest themselves in areas which affect daily living. As an example, people are not likely to know that they have a poor sense of direction until they are old enough to need to ride a bike, drive, or negotiate getting around on their own. An individual who is not very good musically can lead an entire life without being stressed by having a music deficit. Adults have a much better chance of avoiding or circumventing their weaknesses than do children, because students take required courses and adults choose their own careers. Most people choose areas in which they are relatively capable.

Almost everybody has to learn new material at various times in their lives, however, and that is a time when a person might realize the conscious adjustments one is making in order to acquire the knowledge necessary to meet the demand or the expectation. When we learn something new, it may take a little more attention or energy to understand it; sometimes we may have a bit of trouble remembering that which does not quite make sense to us. Maybe we need to hear it again, practice it, or talk it over with a friend or colleague.

These processes are those same ones experienced by children in school. Some children may need to have the instructions repeated, or they may need to be told the directions differently. Some may need to practice the material. Some will forget it, even though they tried to remember it. There are children who try really hard and who become frustrated with themselves because they frequently "do not know what they know they should know." Some of these children withdraw, others behave aggressively. There are students who have medical or neurological or emotional imbalances which interfere with their ability to focus on academic material in the classroom; and there are children whose temperament or whose social environment impedes normal growth and development. All of these unconventional learners need time, patience, and individual understanding. Finding the necessary ingredients to contribute to the child's particular broth is the task at hand for making good soup.

The joy of touching even one hard-to-reach child is a special gratification. When the light goes on in a child's eyes, when a student smiles, when the dawn of recognition delights the youngster, both the child and the teacher share an important bond, a "heart-glow," which will foster further learning and growing. There is no yellow-brick road which leads unerringly to this pot of gold—only a rainbow, a kaleidoscope, of trust, perseverance, integrity, and individuality.

In the end, when I check the thesaurus for the many synonyms for teaching and learning, for teachers, education, intelligence, and scholarship, what I like best are the words which pertain to guiding, discovering, cultivating, and illustrating. These are the "cozy words which feel good," as Brad had described them. Finally, however, it is the wisdom of Einstein which prevails: "Imagination is better than knowledge." Can we risk teaching with creative imagination, individual understanding, flexibility, and sensitivity which foster *the desire to learn*, or must we settle for the scores and percentages which measure specific knowledge?

SUMMARY OF GENERAL ACCOMMODATIONS

IF	THEN
A child seems to be struggling	Ask the child to think aloud so that the problem-solving process can be looked at and described.
A child is not problem solving efficiently	Provide alternate strategies, model new behaviors and tactics, make suggestions for other approaches.
Many individual children need help	Work in groups so as to engage peer aid.
There are many children at different levels of learning	Plan in terms of themes, and allow for individual progress.
A child cannot keep up with written assignments	Engage a helper/recorder, modify the amount to be written.
Children seem to be confused	Break the tasks into small pieces.
Children seem to be haphazard	Help them to understand the process and the steps of organizing tasks.

Help all children to understand how they learn best, and what they can do to facilitate that style of learning.

Encourage all students to evaluate their own weaknesses, and challenge them to come up with learning strategies that will compensate for their deficiencies.

REFERENCE LIST

Bailey, Donald E., Jr., and R. A. McWilliam. (1990) Normalizing early intervention. *Topics in Early Childhood Special Education* 10, no. 2: 33-47.

Clark, Barbara. (1986) *Optimizing Learning: The Integrative Education Model in the Classroom*. Columbus, OH: Merrill Publishing.

Galinsky, Ellen, and Judy David. (1988) *The Preschool Years*. New York: Times Books.

A

Resources Relating to Social-Emotional Issues and Friendships

Asher, S., and P. Renshaw. Children without friends: Social knowledge and social skill training. In: *The Development of Children's Friendships*, Asher & Gottman, eds. New York: Cambridge University Press, 1981, 273-96.

Cheek, J. M., and A. H. Buss. Shyness and sociability. *Journal of Personality and Social Psychology*, 1981, vol. 41: 330-39.

Crary, Elizabeth. *A Children's Problem Solving Book: I Want It*. Seattle: Parenting Press, 1982.

Delisle, James. *Gifted Children Speak Out*. New York: Walker & Co, 1984.

Dowrick, P. *Social Survival for Children*. New York: Brunner/Mazel, 1986.

Fassler, Joan. *Howie Helps Himself*. Chicago: Albert Whitman, 1975.

Field, T., J. Toopnarine, and M. Segal. *Friendships in Normal and Handicapped Children*. Norwood, NJ: Ablex, 1984.

Garrity, Carla. "Children's Friendships Are Important." *St. Anne's Episcopal School Newsletter*, Denver, CO, 1990.

Gottman, J. M. Toward a definition of social isolation in children. *Child Development*, 1977, vol. 48: 513-17.

L'Abete, L., and M. Milan. *A Handbook of Social Skill Training and Research*. New York: Wiley, 1985.

Larsen, Hanne. *Don't Forget Tom*. New York: Crowell, 1978.

Lewis, M., and L. Michalson. *Children's Emotions and Moods*. New York: Plenum Press, 1983.

McGinnis, E., and A. P. Goldstein. *Skillstreaming the Elementary School Child: A Guide for Teaching Prosocial Skills*. Champaign, IL: Research Press, 1984.

Osman, Betty. *No One to Play With*. Novato, CA: Academic Therapy, 1989.

Panek, Dennis. *Matilda Hippo Has a Big Mouth*. Scarsdale, NY: Bradbury, 1980.

Rubin, Zick. *Children's Friendships*. Cambridge, MA: Harvard University Press, 1980.

Saarni, C., and M. Lewis. *The Socialization of Emotions*. New York: Plenum Press, 1985.

Simon, Norma. *Am I Different?* Chicago: Albert Whitman, 1976.

Supraner, Robyn. *It's Not Fair!* New York: Frederick Warne, 1976.

Taylor, A. R. Predictors of peer rejection in early elementary grades: Roles of problem behavior, academic achievement, and teacher preference. *Journal of Clinical Child Psychology*, vol. 18, no. 4: 360-65.

Thomas, A., and S. Chess. *Temperament and Development*. New York: Brunner/Mazel, 1977.

B

Resources for the Language Arts

Atwell, Nancie. *Coming to Know in the Middle*. Portsmouth, NH: Heinemann Publishers, 1987.

Bulletin of the Center for Children's Books. The University of Chicago Press, 5801 Ellis Avenue, Chicago, IL 60637.

Calkins, Lucy. *The Art of Teaching Writing*. Portsmouth, NH: Heinemann Publishers, 1986.

———. *Living between the Lines*. Portsmouth, NH: Heinemann Publishers, 1991.

Cole, Joanna, and Stephanie Calmenson. *The Laugh Book*. Garden City, NY: Doubleday & Company, 1987.

Cullinan, B. E. *Literature and the Child*. New York: Harcourt Brace Jovanovich, 1981.

The Elementary School Library Collection: A Guide to Books and Other Media. Williamsport, PA: Brodart, 1990.

Gibson, Linda. *Literacy Learning in the Early Years through Children's Eyes*. New York: Teachers College Press, 1989.

Graves, Donald H. *Writing: Teachers and Children at Work*. Portsmouth, NH: Heinemann Publishers, 1991.

Hansen, Jane. *When Writers Read*. Portsmouth, NH: Heinemann Publishers, 1987.

Heard, Georgia. *For the Good of the Earth and Sun: Teaching Poetry*. Portsmouth, NH: Heinemann Publishers, 1989.

Huck, C. S. *Children's Literature in the Elementary School*. New York: Holt, Rinehart & Winston, 1979.

Johnson, David W., Roger T. Johnson, Edythe Johnson Holubec, and Patricia Roy. *Circles of Learning: Cooperation in the Classroom*. Alexandria, VA: Association for Supervision and Curriculum Development, 1984.

Paley, Vivian Gussin. *The Boy Who Would Be a Helicopter*. Cambridge, MA: Harvard University Press, 1990.

Phillips, K., and B. Steiner. *Creative Writing: A Handbook for Teaching Young People*. Littleton, CO: Libraries Unlimited, 1985.

The Reading Teacher. International Reading Association, 800 Barksdale Road, P. O. Box 8139, Newark, DE 19714-8139.

Rhodes, L., and Curt Dudley-Marling. *Readers and Writers with a Difference*. Portsmouth, NH: Heinemann Publishers, 1985.

School Library Journal. R. R. Bowker Co., P. O. Box 1426, Riverton, NJ 08077-9967.

Tway, Eileen. *Writing for Reading: 26 Ways to Connect*. Urbana, IL: National Council of Teachers of English, 1985.

Wiig, E., and E. Semel. *Language Disabilities in Children and Adolescents*. Columbus, OH: Charles E. Merrill, 1984.

Williams, Leslie R., ed. *The Early Childhood Education Series*. New York: Teachers College Press.

BASIC SIGHT WORDS

the	when	many	know	there
of	who	before	while	their
and	will	must	last	we
to	more	through	might	him
a	no	back	us	been
in	if	years	great	has
that	out	where	old	man
is	so	much	off	me
was	what	your	come	most
he	said	may	since	made
for	up	well	against	after
it	its	down	go	also
with	about	should	came	did
as	into	because	right	both
his	than	each	used	life
on	them	just	take	being
be	can	those	three	under
at	only	people	himself	never
by	other	Mr.	few	day
I	new	how	house	same

this	some	too	another	use
had	could	little	during	stay
not	time	state	without	high
are	these	good	again	upon
but	two	very	place	school
from	may	take	around	every
or	then	would	however	look
have	do	still	home	ask
an	first	own	small	does
they	any	see	found	got
which	my	men	Mrs.	left
one	now	work	thought	always
you	such	long	went	away
were	like	get	say	hand
her	our	here	part	far
all	over	between	once	took
she				

C

Resources for Mathematics

Anno, Masaichiro, and Mitsumasa Anno. *Anno's Mysterious Multiplying Jar*. New York: Philomel, 1983.

Anno, Mitsumasa. *Anno's Counting House*. New York: Philomel, 1982.

Burns, Marilyn. *The I Hate Mathematics Book*. Boston: Little, Brown & Company, 1975.

_____. *Math for Smarty Pants*. Boston: Little, Brown & Company, 1982.

_____. *A Collection of Math Lessons*. New Rochelle, NY: The Math Solutions Publications, 1987.

Charlesworth, Rosalind, and Deanna Radeloff. *Experiences in Math for Young Children*. Albany, NY: Delmar Publishers, 1991.

Dossey, John A., Ina V.S. Mullis, Mary M. Linquist, and Donald L. Chambers. *The Mathematics Report Card: Are We Measuring Up? Trends and Achievements Based on the 1986 National Assessment*. Princeton, NJ: Educational Testing Service, 1988.

Gag, Wanda. *Millions of Cats*. New York: Coward, McCann & Geoghan, 1977.

Garland, Cynthia. *Math Their Way Summary Newsletters*. Center for Innovation in Education, 1990. (Contains resource list of children's literature.)

130 ■ APPENDIX C

Hutchins, Pat. *The Doorbell Rang*. New York: Greenwillow Book, 1986.

Kellogg, Steven. *Much Bigger Than Martin*. New York: Dial Press, 1976.

Krutetskii, V. A. *The Psychology of Mathematical Abilities in School Children*. Chicago: University of Chicago Press, 1976.

Leutzinger, Larry P., and Myrna Bertheau. Making sense of numbers. In: *New Directions for Elementary School Mathematics*, P. R. Trafton and A. P. Shulte, eds. Reston, VA: National Council of Teachers of Mathematics, 1989.

Lowery, Lawrence. *It's the Thought That Counts*. Palo Alto, CA: Dale Seymour, 1986.

Lundberg, Kristina. *Mathematics Is More Than Counting*. Wheaton, MD: Association for Childhood Education International, 1985.

Mathematics Model Curriculum Guide, K-8. Sacramento, CA: California State Department of Education, 1987.

Mathews, Louise. *Bunches & Bunches of Bunnies*. New York: Scholastic, Inc., 1978.

Moses, Barbara, Elizabeth Bjork, and E. Paul Goldenberg. Beyond problem solving: Problem posing. In: *Teaching and Learning Mathematics in the 1990s*, T. J. Cooney and C. R. Hirsh, eds. Reston, VA: National Council of Teachers of Mathematics, 1990.

Myller, Rolf. *How Big Is a Foot?* Hartford, CT: Atheneum, 1972.

National Council of Teachers of Mathematics. *Mathematics for the Young Child*.

National Research Council. *Everybody Counts*. Washington, DC: National Academy Press, 1989.

Paulos, John Allen. *Innumeracy*. New York: Hill & Wang, 1988.

Rachlin and Ditchburn and Bannon and Sawicki. *First Steps to Mathematics: A Guide for Parents and Teachers to Beginning Mathematics Activities*. Braun & Braun Educational Enterprises, Ltd., 1984.

Richardson, Kathy. *Developing Number Concepts Using Unifix Cubes*. Menlo Park, CA: Addison Wesley, 1984.

Schwartz, David, and Steven Kellogg. *How Much Is a Million?* New York: Lothrop, Lee & Shepard, 1985.

_____. *If You Made a Million*. New York: Lothrop, Lee & Shepard, 1989.

Sharmat, Marjorie Weinman. *The 329th Friend*. New York: Four Winds Press, 1979.

Stenmark, Jean Kerr, Virginia Thompson, and Ruth Cossey. *Family Math*. Berkeley, CA: University of California Press, 1986.

Underhill, R., A. Uprichard, and J. Heddens. *Diagnosing Mathematics Difficulties*. Columbus, OH: Charles E. Merrill, 1980.

Viorst, Judith. *Alexander Who Used to Be Rich Last Sunday*. Hartford, CT: Atheneum, 1978.

_____. *The Tenth Good Thing about Barney*. Hartford, CT: Atheneum, 1978.

Weiss, Sol. *Helping Your Child with Math*. Englewood Cliffs, NJ: Prentice Hall, 1986.

D

Resources for Parents and Teachers

Bloom, Jill. *Help Me to Help My Child.* Boston: Little, Brown, 1990.

Brazelton, T. Berry. *Infants and Mothers.* New York: Dell Publishing, 1969.

Brutten, Milton, Sylvia O. Richardson, and Charles Mangel. *Something's Wrong with My Child.* San Diego: Harcourt Brace Jovanovich Publishers, 1979.

Chinn, P., J. Winn, and R. Walters. *Two-Way Talking with Parents of Special Children.* St. Louis, MO: C. B. Mosby Company, 1978.

Clarke, Louise. *Can't Read, Can't Write, Can't Talk Too Good Either.* New York: Penguin Books, 1974.

Collins, Marva, and Civia Tamarakin. *Marva Collins' Way.* Los Angeles, CA: J. P. Tarcher, 1982.

Comfort, Randy. *The Unconventional Child: A Book for Parents of Children with Learning Difficulties.* Denver, CO: Randy Comfort, 1981.

Craig, Eleanor. *If We Could Hear the Grass Grow.* New York: Simon & Schuster, 1983.

Featherstone, Helen. *A Difference in the Family.* New York: Penguin, 1981.

Fisher, Johanna. *A Parent's Guide to Learning Disabilities*. New York: Scribner's, 1978.

Frey, Karin. Among families of young handicapped children. *Topics in Early Childhood Special Education*, Winter 1989, vol. 8, no. 4: 38.

Granger, Lori, and Bill Granger. *The Magic Feather*. New York: Dutton, 1986.

Jones, Claudia. *Parents Are Teachers Too: Enriching Your Child's First Six Years*. Dayton: Ohio Psychology Press, 1988.

Katz, L. G., J. D. Raths, and R. D. Torres. *A Place Called Kindergarten*. Urbana, IL: Clearing House in Elementary & Early Childhood Education, 1987.

Kroth, Roger. *Communicating with Parents of Exceptional Children*. Denver, CO: Love Publishing, 1975.

Levinson, Harold N. *Smart but Feeling Dumb*. New York: Warner Books, 1984.

MacCracken, Mary. *Turnabout Children*. Boston: Little, Brown, 1986.

Murphy, Albert. *Special Children, Special Parents*. Englewood Cliffs, NJ: Prentice Hall, 1981.

Osman, Betty. *Learning Disabilities, A Family Affair*. New York: Random House, 1979.

Painting, Donald H. *Helping Children with Specific Learning Disabilities: A Practical Guide for Parents and Teachers*. Englewood Cliffs, NJ: Prentice Hall, 1983.

Rosner, Jerome. *Helping Children Overcome Learning Difficulties: A Step-by-Step Guide for Parents and Teachers*. New York: Walker, 1979.

Rothenberg, Mira. *Children with Emerald Eyes*. New York: Dial Press, 1977.

Schoonover, Robert J. *Handbook for Parents of Children with Learning Disabilities*. Danville, IL: Interstate Printers and Publishers, 1983.

Silver, Larry. *The Misunderstood Child*. New York: McGraw-Hill, 1984.

Smith, Sally. *No Easy Answers: The Learning Disabled Child*. New York: Bantam Books, 1987.

Taylor, Barbara. *A Child Goes Forth*. Provo, UT: Brigham Young University Press, 1975.

Turecki, Stanley, and Leslie Tonner. *The Difficult Child*. New York: Bantam Books, 1975.

Turnbull, Ann, and Rutherford Turnbull. *Parents Speak Out*. Columbus, OH: Charles Merrill Publishing Company, 1978.

Weiss, Martin S., and Helen G. Weiss. *Home Is a Learning Place*. Boston: Little, Brown, 1976.

Wikler, Lynn, and Maryanne Keenan. *Developmental Disabilities, No Longer a Private Tragedy*. Silver Spring, MD: National Association of Social Workers, 1983.

GENERAL PARENTING SUPPORT AND INFORMATION AGENCIES

Center for Parent Education, 55 Chapel Street, Newton, MA 02160; 617/964-2442.

Center for Parenting Studies, Wheelock College, 200 The Riverway, Boston, MA 02215; 617/734-5200.

Child Welfare League of America, 440 First Street NW, Washington, DC 20001; 202/638-2952. New York: 212/254-7410.

Family Servce America, 44 East 23rd Street, New York, NY 10010; 212/674-6100.

National Congress of Parents and Teachers, 700 North Rush Street, Chicago, IL 60611; 312/787-0977.

National Parent Center (National Coalition of Title I/Chapter I Parents), 1314 14th Street NW, Suite 6, Washington, DC 20005; 202/483-8822.

National Partnership for Parents' Choice (Institute for Responsive Education), 605 Commonwealth Avenue, Boston, MA 02215; 617/353-3309.

Parents' Rights Organization, 12571 Northwinds Drive, St. Louis, MO 63146; 314/434-4171.

E

General Resource and Reference Information

JOURNALS AND NEWSLETTERS

Closer Look (Newsletter of Parents' Campaign for Handicapped Children and Youth), Box 1492, Washington, DC 20013; 202/822-7900.

Education Daily, 1101 King Street, P. O. Box 1453, Alexandria, VA 22313; 703/683-4100.

Journal of Learning Disabilities, 633 Third Avenue, New York, NY 10017; 212/741-5986.

LD Focus and *LD Research*, Council for Exceptional Children, Division for Learning Disabilities, 1920 Association Drive, Reston, VA 22091; 703/620-3660.

LD Quarterly (Journal of the Council for LD), P. O. Box 40303, Overland Park, KS 66204; 913/492-8755.

EDUCATIONAL MATERIALS

California Association for Neurologically Handicapped Children, Literature Distribution Center, P. O. Box 1526, Vista, CA 92083.

DIALOG Information Services, 340 Hillview Avenue, Palo Alto, CA 94304. (Ask for File 70: special education computer material.)

LINC Resources, Inc. (special education software center), 3857 North High Street, Columbus, OH 43214; 614/263-5462.

National Information Center for Special Education Materials, P.O. Box 40130, Albuquerque, NM 87196.

GUIDES AND DIRECTORIES

Advisory Services on Private Schools and Camps, 171 Madison Avenue, New York, NY 10016; 212/696-0499.

BOSC Directory for Facilities for Learning Disabled, Department F, Box 305, Congers, NY 10920.

Guide to Summer Camps and Summer Schools, Porter Sargent Publications, 11 Beacon Street, Boston, MA 02108.

Handbook of Private Schools, Porter Sargent Publications, 11 Beacon Street, Boston, MA 02108.

National Association of Private Schools for Exceptional Children: Membership Directory, NAPSEC, 2021 K Street, Suite 315, Washington, DC 20006.

Schooling for the Learning Disabled: A Selective Guide to LD Programs in Elementary and Secondary Schools in the U.S., Raegene Pernecke and Sara M. Schrenier, SMS Publishing Corporation, P. O. Box 2276, Glenview, IL 60025.

NATIONAL SPECIAL NEEDS AND ADVOCACY ORGANIZATIONS

Association for Children with Learning Disabilities (National Headquarters), 4156 Library Road, Pittsburgh, PA 15243; 412/341-1515.

Center for Law and Education, 236 Massachusetts Avenue NE, Suite 504, Washington, DC 20002; 202/546-5300.

Children's Defense Fund, 122 C Street NW, Washington, DC 20001; 202/628-8787.

Children's Foundation, 1028 Connecticut Avenue NW, Washington, DC 20036.

Closer Look/Parents' Campaign for Handicapped Children and Youth, 1201 Sixteenth Street NW, Washington, DC 20036; 202/833-4160 or 202/822-7900.

Council for Exceptional Children, 1920 Association Drive, Reston, VA 22091; 703/620-3660.

Council for Learning Disabilities, P. O. Box 40303, Overland Park, KS 66204; 913/492-8755.

Federation for Children with Special Needs (National Network of Parents), 312 Stuart Street, Boston, MA 02116; 617/482-2915.

Foundation for Children with Learning Disabilities (National Foundation for Learning Disabilities), 99 Park Avenue, New York, NY 10016.

National Association for the Education of Young Children, 1834 Connecticut Avenue NW, Washington, DC 20009.

National Coalition of Advocates for Students, 76 Summer Street, Boston, MA 02100; 617/357-8507.

Orton Dyslexia Society (National Headquarters), 724 York Road, Baltimore, MD 21204; 301/296-0232.

U.S. Department of Education, Office of Special Education and Rehabilitative Services, 330 C Street SW, Room 3006, Washington, DC 20202.

Bibliography

Able-Boone, Harriet. An Informed, Family-Centered Approach to Public Law 99-457. *Topics in Early Childhood Special Education* 10, no. 1 (Spring 1990): 100.

Adams, M. J. *Beginning to Read*. Cambridge, MA: MIT Press, 1990.

Allen, K. Eileen. *Mainstreaming in Early Childhood Education*. New York: Delmar Publishers, 1980.

Almy, Millie. *The Early Childhood Educator at Work*. New York: McGraw-Hill, 1975.

Ayers, William. *The Good PreSchool Teacher*. New York: Teachers College Press, 1986.

Bailey, Donald E., Jr., and R. A. McWilliam. Normalizing Early Intervention. *Topics in Early Childhood Special Education* 10, no. 2 (1990): 33-47.

Bauer, Hanna. *Beyond Instruction in Special Education*. Novato, CA: Academic Therapy Publications, 1977.

Berndt, Thomas. Quoted by Elizabeth Schultz, Research. *Teaching and Learning* (November 1989): 34.

Bloom, Jill. *Help Me to Help My Child*. Boston: Little, Brown, 1990.

Bloom, Lois, and M. Lahey, *Language Development and Language Disorders*. New York: Wiley, 1978.

Boslough, John. *Stephen Hawking's Universe*. New York: Quill/William Morrow, 1985.

Bransford, J., and M. Johnson. Contextual Prerequisites for Understanding: Some Investigation of Comprehension and Recall. *Journal of Verbal Learning and Verbal Behavior* 11 (1972): 726-27.

Brazelton, T. Berry. *Infants and Mothers*. New York: Dell Publishing, 1969.

Brobeck, Joyce K. Teachers Do Make a Difference. *Journal of Learning Disabilities* 23, no. 1 (January 1990): 11-12.

Brooks, Robert. Learning Disabilities from the Perspective of a Clinical Psychologist. Paper presented at New England Joint Conference on Specific Learning Disabilities, 1987.

Brown, Catherine Caldwell, ed. Childhood Learning Disabilities and Prenatal Risk. Paper presented at Johnson & Johnson Baby Products' Pediatric Round Table Discussion, Skillman, NJ, 1983.

Brutten, Milton, Sylvia O. Richardson, and Charles Mangel. *Something's Wrong with My Child*. San Diego: Harcourt Brace Jovanovich Publishers, 1979.

Buscaglia, L. Parents Need to Know: Parents and Teachers Working Together. In: *Learning Disabilities: Selected ACLD Papers*. Edited by S. Kirk and J. McCarthy. Boston: Houghton Mifflin, 1975.

Camp, B. W., and M. A. Bash. *Think Aloud: Increasing Social and Cognitive Skills—A Problem Solving Program for Children*. Champaign, IL: Research Press, 1981.

Caspi, Avshalom, Glen H. Elder Jr., and Daryl J. Bem. Moving against the World: Life-Course Patterns of Explosive Children. *Developmental Psychology* 22 (1987): 303-08.

_____. Moving Away from the World: Life-Course Patterns of Shy Children. *Developmental Psychology* 24, no. 6 (1988): 824-31.

Chall, Jeanne S. *Learning to Read: The Great Debate*. New York: McGraw-Hill, 1967.

———. *Stages of Reading Development*. New York: McGraw-Hill, 1983.

Chance, Paul. "Kids without Friends." *Psychology Today* 23, no. 1 (January/February 1989).

Chess, S., and A. Thomas. *Annual Progress in Child Psychiatry and Child Development*. New York: Brunner/Mazel, 1983 and 1984.

Clark, Barbara. *Optimizing Learning: The Integrative Education Model in the Classroom*. Columbus, OH: Merrill Publishing, 1986.

Clark, D. B. *Dyslexia: Theory & Practice of Remedial Instruction*. Parkton, MD: York Press, 1988.

Clark, Louise. *Can't Read, Can't Write, Can't Talk Too Good Either*. New York: Penguin Books, 1974.

Coles, Gerald. *The Learning Mystique*. New York: Pantheon Books, 1987.

Comfort, Randy Lee. *The Unconventional Child*. 1330 Leyden St., Denver, CO 80220, 1980.

———. *The Child Care Catalog*. Littleton, CO: Libraries Unlimited, 1985.

———. Cognitive-Affective Discrepancies in Three Gifted Boys. Ph.D. diss., University of Denver, CO, 1988.

Cruickshank, W., F. Bentzen, F. Ratzeburg, and M. Tannhauser. *A Teaching Method for Brain-Injured and Hyperactive Children*. Syracuse, NY: Syracuse University Press, 1961.

Cruickshank, William. *Learning Disabilities in Home, School, and Community*. Syracuse, NY: Syracuse University Press, 1977.

Cummings, Rhoda Woods, and Cleborne D. Maddox. *Parenting the Learning Disabled Child*. Springfield, IL: C. C. Thomas, 1985.

DeRuiter, J. A., and W. L. Wansart. *Psychology of Learning Disabilities: Applications and Educational Practices*. Rockville, MD: Aspen, 1982.

Deutsch, D., ed. *The Psychology of Music*. London: Academic Press, 1982.

Dimidjian, Victoria Jean. *Early Childhood at Risk*. Washington, DC: National Education Association of the U.S., 1989.

Edwards, Carolyn Pope. *Promoting Social and Moral Development in Young Children*. New York: Teachers College Press, 1986.

Emde, R., T. Gaensbauer, and R. Harmon. Using Our Emotions: Some Principles for Appraising Emotional Development and Intervention. In: *Developmental Disabilities: Theory, Assessment, and Intervention*. Edited by M. Lewis and I. Tafts. New York: S. P. Medical and Scientific Books, 1982.

Erickson, Tim. *Get It Together*. Berkeley, CA: Lawrence Hall of Science, 1989.

Feagans, L., B. Short, and L. Meltzer, eds. *Learning Disability Subtypes*. Hillsdale, NJ: Erlbaum, 1990.

Feuerstein, R., V. Rand, M. Hoffman, and R. Miller. *Instrumental Enrichment: An Intervention Program for Cognitive Modifiability*. Baltimore: University Park Press, 1980.

Fisher, Johanna. *A Parent's Guide to Learning Disabilities*. New York: Scribner's, 1978.

Fitzgerald, J. *A Basic Life Spelling Vocabulary*. Milwaukee, WI: Bruce, 1951.

Fox, L., L. Brody, and D. Tobin. *Learning Disabled/Gifted Children*. Baltimore: University Park Press, 1983.

Franklin, Barry M. *Learning Disabilities: Dissenting Views*. Philadelphia: The Palmer Press, 1987.

Frey, K. S., R. R. Fewell, and P. F. Vadasy. Parental Adjustment and Changes in Child Outcome among Families of Young Handicapped Children. *Topics in Early Childhood Special Education* 8, no. 4 (1989): 38-57.

Frey, Karin. Among Families of Young Handicapped Children. *Topics in Early Childhood Special Education* 8, no. 4 (Winter 1989): 38.

Galinsky, Ellen, and Judy David. *The Preschool Years*. New York: Times Books, 1988.

Gardner, Howard. *Frames of Mind*. New York: Basic Books, 1983.

Gearheart, Bill. *Learning Disabilities: Educational Strategies*. St. Louis: C. V. Mosby Company, 1981.

Gilligan, Carol. *In a Different Voice*. Cambridge, MA: Harvard University Press, 1982.

Ginott, Haim G. *Between Parent and Child*. New York: Avon Books, 1971.

Goodlad, John. *A Place Called School: Prospects for the Future*. New York: McGraw-Hill, 1984.

Goodman, Ken. *What's Whole in Whole Language?* Portsmouth, NH: Heinemann Educational Books, 1986.

Gordon, Thomas. *Parent Effectiveness Training*. New York: New American Library, 1975.

Granger, Lori, and Bill Granger. *The Magic Feather*. New York: Dutton, 1986.

Greenspan, Stanley. *Psychopathology and Adaptation in Infancy and Early Childhood*. New York: International Universities Press, 1981.

_____. Fostering Emotional and Social Development in Infants with Disabilities. *Zero to Three* 9, no. 1 (September 1988).

Guralnick, Michael. Mainstreaming Young Handicapped Children: A Public Policy and Ecological Systems Analysis. In: *Handbook of Research in Early Childhood Education*. Edited by Bernard Spodek. New York: The Free Press, 1982.

Haber, Julian, M.D., and Florence Isaacs. "Helping Learning Disabled Children." *Good Housekeeping* 209, no. 3 (September 1989): 162.

Hohmann, Gary, Bernard Banet, and David Weikart. *Young Children in Action*. Ypsilanti, MI: High/Scope Press, 1979.

Holt, John. *Learning All the Time*. New York: Addison-Wesley Publishing, 1989.

Hutchins, Pat. *Changes, Changes*. New York: Macmillan, 1987.

Hyman, Irwin. *Reading, Writing and the Hickory Stick*. Lexington, MA: Lexington Books, 1990.

Jaquez-Dalcroze, E. *Rhythm, Music and Education*. Pyrford, England: The Dalcroze Society, 1921, revised 1967.

Johnson, David W., Roger T. Johnson, Edythe Johnson Holubec, and Patricia Roy. *Circles of Learning: Cooperation in the Classroom*. Alexandria, VA: Association for Supervision and Curriculum Development, 1984.

Johnson-Martin, Nancy, Susan Attermeier, and Bonnie Hacker. *The Carolina Curriculum for PreSchoolers with Special Needs*. Baltimore: Paul Brookes Publishing Co., 1990.

Jones, Claudia. *Parents Are Teachers Too: Enriching Your Child's First Six Years*. Dayton: Ohio Psychology Press, 1988.

Jones, Malinda, Karen Daves, and Cathy Kurkjian. Observation in the Classroom: What It Takes. *The Colorado Communicator* (November 1990): 36-41.

Kamii, Constance. *Young Children Reinvent Arithmetic*. New York and London: Teachers College Press, 1985.

———. *Young Children Continue to Reinvent Arithmetic*. New York and London: Teachers College Press, 1989.

Katz, L. G., J. D. Raths, and R. D. Torres. *A Place Called Kindergarten*. Urbana, IL: Clearing House in Elementary & Early Childhood Education, 1987: 29.

Kirk, S. Behavioral Diagnosis and Remediation of Learning Disabilities. Paper presented at Conference on the Exploration into the Problems of the Perceptually Handicapped Child, Evanston, IL, 1963.

Kirk, Samuel, ed. *Learning Disabilities: Selected ACLD Papers*. Boston: Houghton Mifflin, 1975.

Kistner, Janet, Frank Robbins, and Mary Haskett. Assessment and Skill Remediation of Hyperlexic Children. *Journal of Autism and Developmental Disorders* 18, no. 2 (June 1988): 191-205.

Kronick, Doreen. *New Approaches to Learning Disabilities*. Philadelphia: Greene and Stratton, 1988.

Lerner, Janet. *Children with Learning Disabilities: Theory, Diagnoses, Teaching Strategies*. Boston: Houghton Mifflin, 1976.

_____. *Learning Disabilities*. Boston: Houghton Mifflin, 1985.

Lerner, Janet, Carol Mardell-Czudnowski, and Dorothea Goldenberg. *Special Education for the Early Childhood Years*. Englewood Cliffs, NJ: Prentice Hall, 1987.

Levine, M. Common Development Dysfunctions in School Children. Cambridge, MA: Educators Publishing Service, 1983.

Levine, M. D., and P. Satz, eds. *Middle Childhood, Development and Dysfunction*. Baltimore: University Park Press, 1984: 131-52.

Levine, Mel. *Attention Deficit Disorders: The Diverse Effects of Weak Control Systems in Childhood*. Cambridge, MA: Educators Publishing Service, 1986.

Levine, Melvin. *Developmental Variation and Learning Disabilities*. Cambridge, MA: Educators Publishing Service, 1987.

_____. *Keeping a Head in School*. Cambridge, MA: Educators Publishing Service, 1990.

Levine, Melvin D., Robert Brooks, and J. Shonkoff. *A Pediatric Approach to Learning Disorders*. New York: John Wiley & Sons, 1980.

Levinson, Harold N. *Smart but Feeling Dumb*. New York: Warner Books, 1984.

Lewis, Georgia. Books for the Classroom Teacher: Some Practical Selections. *Childhood Education* 62, no. 2 (November/December 1985): 122-26.

Lewis, Rena. *Teaching Special Students in the Mainstream*. Columbus, OH: Charles Merrill, 1983.

Lloyd, J. W., E. P. Crowley, F. W. Kohler, and P. S. Strain. Redefining the Applied Research Agenda: Cooperative Learning Prereferral, Teacher Consultation, and Peer Mediated Interventions. *Journal of Learning Disabilities* 21, no. 1 (1988): 43-52.

Luria, A. R. *The Mind of a Mnemonist*. Cambridge, MA: Harvard University Press, 1987.

MacCoby, Eleanor E., Norman Garmezy, and Michael Rutter, eds. Social Emotional Development and Response to Stressors. In: *Stress, Coping, and Development in Children*. New York: McGraw-Hill, 1983, pp. 217-33.

MacCracken, Mary. *Turnabout Children*. Boston: Little, Brown, 1986.

Mastropieri, M., T. Scruggs, and S. Shiah. Mathematics Instruction for Learning Disabled Students: A Review of Research. *Learning Disabilities Research and Practice* 6, no. 2 (1991): 89-99.

McGinnis, E., and A. P. Goldstein. *Skillstreaming the Elementary School Child: A Guide for Teaching Prosocial Skills*. Champaign, IL: Research Press, 1984.

McKinney, James, and Lynne Feagan. *Current Topics in Learning Disabilities*. Norwood, NY: Ablex Publishing, 1983.

McLean, Mary. Providing Early Intervention Services in Integrated Environments: Challenges and Opportunities for the Future. *Topics in Early Childhood Special Education* 10, no. 2 (1990): 62-77.

Meltzer, L. J., B. Solomon, and T. Fenton. Problem-solving Strategies in Children with and without Learning Disabilities. Paper presented at the 95th Annual Convention of the American Psychological Association, New York, August 1987.

Meltzer, Lynn. Problem-solving Strategies and Academic Performance in Learning Disabled Students: Do Subtypes Exist? In: *Learning Disability Subtypes*. Edited by L. Feagans, B. Short, and L. Meltzer. Hillsdale, NJ: Erlbaum, 1990.

Meltzer, Lynn, and Bethany Solomon. *Educational Prescriptions for the Classroom for Students with Learning Problems*. Cambridge, MA: Educators Publishing, 1988.

Mitchell, Anne, Michelle Seligson, and Fern Marx. *Early Childhood Programs and the Public Schools*. Boston, MA: Auburn House, 1989.

Morrison, George. *Early Childhood Education Today*. Columbus, OH: Charles E. Merrill Publishing, 1984.

Morrow, Lance. The Bright Cave under the Hat. *Time* 136, no. 27 (December 24, 1990): 78.

National Association for the Education of Young Children. *Good Teaching Practices for 4 and 5 Year Olds*. NAEYC Position Paper, Washington, DC, 1986.

Oden, S., and S. Asher. Coaching Children in Social Skills for Friendship Making. *Child Development* 48 (1977): 495-506.

Odom, S. L., and M. A. McEvoy. Mainstreaming at the Preschool Level: Potential Barriers and Tasks for the Field. *Topics in Early Childhood Special Education* 10, no. 2 (1990): 48-61.

Osman, Betty. *Learning Disabilities: A Family Affair*. New York: Random House, 1979.

———. *The Social Side of Learning Disabilities*. New York: Random House, 1982.

———. *No One to Play With*. Novato, CA: Academic Therapy, 1989.

Painting, Donald H. *Helping Children with Specific Learning Disabilities: A Practical Guide for Parents and Teachers*. Englewood Cliffs, NJ: Prentice Hall, 1983.

Palincsar, A. S., and A. L. Brown. Reciprocal Teaching of Comprehension—Fostering and Monitoring Activities. *Cognition and Instruction* 1 (1984): 117-75.

Paulos, John Allen. *Innumeracy*. New York: Hill and Wang, 1988.

Pavlidis, George, and Dennis Fisher, eds. *Dyslexia: Its Neuropsychology and Treatment*. New York: John Wiley & Sons, 1986.

Piaget, J. *The Origins of Intelligence in Children*. New York: International University Press, 1952.

_____. *The Language and Thought of the Child*. New York: World Publishing, 1962.

_____. *The Child's Conception of Number*. New York: W. W. Norton, 1965.

Pinnell, Gay Su, Mary D. Fried, and Rose Mary Estice. Reading Recovery: Learning How to Make a Difference. *The Reading Teacher* 43, no. 4 (January 1990): 282-95.

Postman, Neil. *The Disappearance of Childhood*. New York: Delacorte, 1982.

Preis, Sandra, and George Cocks. *Arithmetic*. Englewood Cliffs, NJ: Prentice Hall, 1990.

Rachlin, Jill. "Labeling away Problem Kids: Are Learning Disabilities a Medical Fact or a Convenient Fiction?" *U.S. News & World Report* 106, no. 3 (March 13, 1989): 59.

Ramsey, Patricia G. Teaching and Learning in a Diverse World: Multicultural Education. *Early Childhood Education Series*. Edited by Leslie R. Williams, 1987.

Reid, Kim. *Teaching the Learning Disabled*. Boston: Allyn & Bacon, 1988.

_____. N.t. Paper presented at Denver Academy Lecture, Denver, CO, 1990.

Reid, Kim and Wayne Hresko. *A Cognitive Approach to Learning Disabilities*. New York: McGraw-Hill, 1981.

Rimm, Sylvia. *Underachievement Syndrome: Causes and Cures*. Dayton: Ohio Psychology Press, 1989.

Ritchhart, Ronald. *Exploring Our Numeracy: Moving Beyond Number Sense*. Master's Thesis, University of Colorado, 1991; Addison-Wesley, forthcoming.

Robertson, Glenda F., and Mary A. Johnson. *Leaders in Education: Their Views on Controversial Issues*. New York: University Press of America, 1988.

Robison, H. F. *Exploring Teaching in Early Childhood Education*. Boston: Allyn & Bacon, 1977.

Roedell, Wendy C. Vulnerabilities of Highly Gifted Children. *Roeper Review* 6, no. 3 (February 1984): 127-30.

Rogers, Sally J. Cognitive Characteristics of Handicapped Children's Play: A Review. *Journal of the Division of Early Childhood* 12, no. 2 (1988).

Rule, S., B. J. Frechtl, and M. S. Innocenti. Preparation for Transition to Mainstreamed Post-Preschool Environments: Development of a Survival Skills Curriculum. *Topics in Early Childhood Special Education* 9, no. 4 (Winter 1990): 78.

Sacks, Oliver. *The Man Who Mistook His Wife for a Hat*. New York: Harper & Row, 1987.

Safford, Philip. *Integrated Teaching in Early Childhood*. New York: Congman, 1989.

Saint Exupery, Antoine de. *The Little Prince*. New York: Harcourt Brace & World, 1943.

Schattner, Regina. *An Early Childhood Curriculum for Multiply Handicapped Children*. New York: The John Day Co., 1991.

Schoonover, Robert J. *Handbook for Parents of Children with Learning Disabilities*. Danville, IL: Interstate Printers and Publishers, 1983.

Seefeldt, Carol. Who Meets the Standards for Early Childhood Teachers. *The Education Digest* (May 1, 1989).

Senior, Eileen M. Learning Disabled or Merely Mislabeled? The Plight of the Developmentally Young Child. *Childhood Education* 62, no. 3 (January/February 1986): 161-65.

Shannon, Patrick. *Broken Promises.* New York: Bergin & Garvey, 1989.

Sharmat, Marjorie. *Big Fat Enormous Lie.* New York: Dutton, 1978.

Short, E. J., and E. B. Ryan. Metacognitive Differences between Skilled and Less Skilled Readers: Remediating Deficits through Story Grammar and Attribution Training. *Journal of Educational Psychology* 76 (1984): 225-35.

Short, E. J., and J. Weissberg-Benchell. The Triple Alliance for Learning: Cognition, Metacognition and Motivation. In: *Cognitive Strategy Research: From Basic Research to Educational Applications.* Edited by C. McCormich, G. Miller, and M. Pressley. New York: Springer-Verlag, 1989: 33-63.

Short, E. J., C. L. Cuddy, S. E. Friebert, and C. Schatschneider. The Diagnostic and Educational Utility of Thinking Aloud during Problem Solving. In: *Learning Disabilities: Theoretical Research Issues.* Edited by L. Swanson and B. Keogh. Hillsdale, NJ: Lawrence Erlbaum Associates, 1990.

Siegel, Linda S., and Bruce A. Linder. Short-Term Memory Processes in Children with Reading and Arithmetic Learning Disabilities. *Developmental Psychology* 20, no. 2 (March 1984): 200-207.

Silver, Larry. *The Misunderstood Child.* New York: McGraw-Hill, 1984.

Smith, E. Brooks, Kenneth Goodman, and Robert Meredith. *Language and Thinking in School.* New York: Holt, Rinehart and Winston, 1976.

Smith, Sally. *No Easy Answers: The Learning Disabled Child.* New York: Bantam Books, 1987.

Spodek, Bernard. *Handbook of Research in Early Childhood Education.* New York: Free Press, 1982.

Stegner, Wallace. *Two Rivers*. In: *Collected Stories of Wallace Stegner*. New York: Random House, 1990.

Stevens, Suzanne H. *Classroom Success for the Learning Disabled*. Winston-Salem, NC: John F. Blair, 1984.

_____. *How to Rescue At-Risk Students*. Winston-Salem, NC: LDTV, 1990.

Swanson, H. L. Learning Disabled Children's Problem Solving: Identifying Mental Processes underlying Intelligent Performance. *Intelligence* 12, no. 3 (1988): 261-78.

_____. Strategy Instruction: Overview of Principles and Procedures for Effective Use. *Learning Disability Quarterly* 12, no. 1 (1989): 3-14.

Swanson, Lee, and Barbara Keogh. *Learning Disabilities: Theoretical Research Issues*. Hillsdale, NJ: Lawrence Erlbaum Associates, 1990.

Taylor, Barbara. *A Child Goes Forth*. Provo, UT: Brigham Young University Press, 1975.

Taylor, Dorothy. *Physical Movement and Memory for Music* 6, no. 3 (1989): 251-60. Edited by B. J. Music, Great Britain.

Thomas, A., and S. Chess. *Temperament and Development*. New York: Brunner/Mazel, 1977.

Tobias, Sheila. *Succeed with Math*. New York: College Board Publications, 1987.

Torgesen, J. K. Performance of Reading Disabled Children on Serial Memory Tasks: A Selective Review of Recent Research. *Reading Research Quarterly* 14 (1978): 57-87.

_____. The Learning Disabled Child as an Inactive Learner: Educational Implications. *Topics in Learning and Learning Disabilities* 2, no. 1 (1982): 45-51.

Torgesen, J. K., and B. Licht. The Learning-disabled Child as an Inactive Learner: Retrospects and Prospects. In: *Current Topics in Learning Difficulties* 1: 3-31. Edited by J. McKinney and L. Feagans. Norwood, NJ: Ablex, 1983.

Towsend, Lena O. Is Your Child Learning Disabled? *Essence Magazine* 20, no. 1 (October 1989): 118.

Turecki, Stanley, and Leslie Tonner. *The Difficult Child*. New York: Bantam Books, 1985.

Uzgiris, Ina C., J. McV. Hunt. *Assessment in Infancy*. Urbana: University of Illinois Press, 1975.

Vail, Priscilla. *Smart Kids with School Problems*. New York: Dutton, 1987.

Vygotsky, L. *Thought and Language*. Cambridge, MA: MIT Press, 1962.

Wagner, Richard, and Janet Kistner. Implications of the Distinction between Academic and Practical Intelligence for Learning Disabled Children. In: *Learning Disabilities*. Edited by L. Swanson and B. Keogh. Hillsdale, NJ: Lawrence Erlbaum, 1990: 76.

Weiss, Martin S., and Helen G. Weiss. *Home Is a Learning Place*. Boston: Little, Brown, 1976.

Winton, P. J. Promoting a Normalizing Approach to Families: Integrating Theory with Practice. *Topics in Early Childhood Special Education* 10, no. 2 (1990): 90-103.

Index

Accommodations
   for classroom teachers, 109-21
   learning dysfunctions, ix
   on specific assignments, 118
   strategies for teaching and learning, 44-48
Active learning, 46-47
   asking questions, 46
   discovery learning, 46-47
Active memory, 18
Adaptations for classroom teachers, 109-21
Allergies, 26
Almy, Millie, 103
Aphasia, 2
Associative information storage, 17
Attention deficits, 36
Atwell, Nanci, 63
Auditorial tasks, 20
Auditory perception, 14-15
Auditory processing difficulties, 8, 65, 68

Bailey, Donald E., Jr., 111
Basal readers, 65
Behavior, 8, 29-31, 32
   management, 42-44
   observations, 10, 24
   social interactions, 42
   styles, 43
Behavior modification, 44
Berndt, Thomas, 27
The Big Fat Enormous Lie, 87

Body regulation problems, 25
Boys vs. girls with learning difficulties, 8
Brain injury, 2
Bransford, J., 60
Brazelton, T. Berry, 13
Broad-based learning deficits, 49-50(table 4.1)
Brown, Catherine Caldwell, 59
Brutten, Milton, 3
Buddy system, 39, 117

Calkins, Lucy, 63
Can't Read, Can't Write, Can't Talk Too Good Either, 3
Caregiver and child relationship, 35
Cause-and-effect, 88
Cerebral palsy, 4, 56, 109
Chall, Jeanne S., 59
Chance, Paul, 27
Changes, Changes, 87
Charts for organizing, 117
Chess, S., 25
Child development stages, 70
Chunking, 17
Clark, Barbara, 111
Clark, Louise, 3
Classrooms
   adapting to meet individual needs, 111-21
   environment, 111-12
   normalization, 111
Cloze method, 69

156 ■ INDEX

Cognition, 24-25
   approach to learning difficulties, 48
   and functional deficiency, 23
   and language deficits, 56
Cognitive-affective discrepancies, 42
Common Development Dysfunctions in School Children, 48
Communication between parents and teachers, 107-8
Concept learning, 39
Contextual reading, 114
Coordinated processing, 45-46
Counting skills, 80, 94-96
Cruickshank, W. F., 36

Darwin, Charles, 6
David, Judy, 111
Day care and child relationship, 35
Developmental differences, 3, 22-33, 36, 104
   behavior, 29-31
   cognition, 24-25
   learning deficits, 23-24
   social-emotional development, 27-28
   strategies, 32
   temperament, 25-26
The Difficult Child, 3, 104
Directionality problems, 113-14
Discovery learning, 46-47
Drill and skill exercises, 63-64
Dyslexia, 2
Dyslexics, 64, 76
   reading programs, 59
Dysynchrony, 30

Early identification of learning delays, 30
Edison, Thomas, 6
Education for All Handicapped Children Act (1975), Public Law 94-142, 2, 3
Education of the Handicapped Act Amendments (1986), Public Law 99-455, 3
Educational deficit, 8
Educational Prescriptions for the Classroom, 48
Emde, R. T., 26

Emotional problems, 27
   and learning delays, 30
Environment
   and classrooms, 111
   demands of, 26
   and reading, 60
Estimating in math, 88-90
Expressive language, 55, 94

Feagans, L., 46
Fenton, T., 46
Feuerstein, Reuven, 25
Fine motor weakness, 76
   numeracy deficits, 98
Friendships, 27

Galileo, 6
Galinsky, Ellen, 111
Games in math, 90-91
Gender differences, learning difficulties, 8
Generalizing, numeracy, 85
Gestalt, 17, 62
Ginott, Haim G., 106
Goldilocks, 87
Gordon, Thomas, 106
Graves, Donald, 63
Greenspan, Stanley, 26, 36
Grouping, 94-96

Haber, Julian, 2
Hansen, Jane, 63
Hawking, Stephen, 19-20
Heard, Georgia, 63
Hearing impairment, 56
Hemingway, Ernest, 6
Hidden handicaps, 102
Holt, John, 80
Home life, disadvantaged, 104-5
Houghton Mifflin, 65
Hresko, Wayne, 45
Hunt, J. McV., 56

I messages, 106
Immaturity, 27
Impulsivity, 9

Inactive learners, 46
Individualized approach, 37, 118-19
Inefficient learners, 38
Inefficient problem-solving strategies, 47
Information processing, 16-19
Information remembering, 18-19
Information storage
  associative, 17
  linking, 17
  rules, 17
Inner language, 55
Innumeracy, 79. *See also* Numeracy
Input
  auditory perception, 14-15
  sensory perception, 15
  social perception, 16
  visual perception, 14
Instruction method adjustments, 45
Integrated educational approach, 44-45, 112
Intellectual progress, 111
Interactional learning, 42
Interactional purpose of language, 55
Interviewing the child, 61
Investigative learning in math, 81

James, William, 18
Johnson, David W., 60

Kamii, Constance, 80, 81, 91
Katz, L. G., 35
Kirk, Samuel, 2
Kistner, Janet, 42
Kraus, Robert, 58
Kronick, Doreen, 43

Labels, 3-4, 102
Language
  and auditory deficits and phonics, 61
  and cognition connection, 55, 56
  communication, 54-66
    preschool and kindergarten, 57-58
  delays and numeracy deficits, 98
  intervention, 69
  processing, 68-69
  and sight/sound-symbol relationships, 70
Language dysfunctions, 10, 21, 56, 57, 76-77, 84-85
  first or second grade, 58-59
  identifying or recognizing, 75-77
  middle school age, 59
  and neurological disorders, 56
  possible indications, 75
Language experience reading programs, 65
Learning abilities, 37
Learning deficits, 23-24
  cognitive capacity and functional deficiency, 23
  demystifying, 30
Learning difficulties, boys vs. girls, 8
Learning disabilities
  accommodation in regular classroom, ix
  defining, 2-5
  emotional vulnerability as secondary symptoms, 7
  hidden handicaps, 7
  historical figures with, 6
  labels, 3-4
  legislation, 2-3
  misdiagnosed and undiagnosed, 7
  official identification, 6
  older elementary child, 6
  preschool years, 6
  standardized testing, 7-8
  uncertainty, 101-8
  variant learning behaviors, 5
Learning Disabilities Association Membership Services Committee, 2
Learning process, 12-21
  input, 13-16
  output, 19-20
  and problem-solving, 38-42
  processing and remembering, 16-19
  strategies, 20-21
Learning styles, 5, 32, 36
Least restrictive environment, 3
Legislation for children with disabilities, 2-3
Leo the Late Bloomer, 58
Less-adaptive child, 26
Levine, Melvin, 3, 16, 38, 48

Linguistics reading programs, 65
Linking, information storage, 17
Literacy behaviors, 44
Living problems, ix, 39
Logical reasoning, 96-97
Long-term memory, 18
Luria, A. R., 18

Mainstreaming, 34-35, 37, 115
Maladaptive learners, 38
The Man Who Mistook His Wife for a Hat, 18
Manipulatives, numeracy deficits, 99
Mathematical literacy, 79. *See also* Numeracy
Mathematics, 78-99
   learning disabilities and, 82
   lesson examples, 94-97
   numeracy, 79-92
   recognizing dysfunctions, 97-99
   and spelling abilities, 30
   teaching strategies, 92-97
Measuring, 89, 90
Meltzer, Lynn, 38, 46, 48
Memorization, 41, 62, 68
Memory, 18-19
   abilities, 92
   deficits, 18, 21, 41, 77
   and numeracy deficits, 98-99
Metacognitive processes, 38, 88
Middle school age, language deficits, 59
The Mind of a Mnemonist, 18
The Misunderstood Child, 104
Mitchell, Anne, 35
Morrison, George, 30, 37
Morrow, Lance, 104
Motor abilities, 21
Motor-based activities, 87
Motor output, 19
Motor planning, 19, 21
Multicultural children, 31
Multisensory reading programs, 65-66
Multisensory teaching, 20, 58, 76
Mutual storytelling, 57
Mutuality, 19

NAEYC. *See* National Association of Education for Young Children
National Association of Education for Young Children (NAEYC), 36-37
Neurological disorders, 56
No Easy Answers: The Learning Disabled Child, 3
No One to Play With, 27
Non-linguistic communication, 57
Normalization, 111
Number concepts, 79-80, 98-99
Numeracy, 79-92
   analyzing data, 91
   games, 90-91
   generalizing, 85
   graphing, 91
   identifying what data to collect, 91
   making connections, 85
   problem-solving, 82, 91
   seriation, 87
   temporal or visual sequential deficits, 83
   whole language/language experience, 85
Numeracy deficits, 98-99
   fine motor weakness, 98
   language delays, 98
   manipulatives, 99
   memory deficits, 98, 99
   number concept weaknesses, 98-99
   possible indications, 97-98
   problem-solving approaches, 99
   sequencing difficulties, 98
   visual motor weaknesses, 98

Observation record of child's behavior, 48
One-to-one correspondence, 86, 87
Orton-Gillingham reading program, 65
The Orton Society, 59
Osman, Betty, 27
Output, 19-20
   dysfunctions, 19-20
   motor output, 19
   motor planning, 19
Over-reading social interactions, 16

Palincsar, A. S., 59
Parents
　attitudes about temperament, 26
　behavior observation, 9
　defining learning disabilities, 3
　and family interaction, 104
　and teachers, 101-8
　and teachers communication, 107-8
Participatory learning, 48
Partnership plan with students, 117
Paulos, John Allen, 79
Peers
　appropriate behavior, 43
　differences, 42
　relationship problems, 10
　working together, 118
Perceptual difficulties, 14
Phonics
　reading programs, 65
　strategies, 64
　weakness, 59
Piaget, J., 35
Place value concepts, 83, 84, 87-88, 96-97
Preoperational thought, 55
Preschool children
　diagnosis, 8
　group setting, 3
　teachers, 87
Problem solving, 46, 50, 105, 111
　inefficient strategies, 47
　model approach, 46
　numeracy deficits, 99
　strategies, 38-40
Processing, 16-19, 21
　deficits, 13, 20
Public Law 94-142, Education for All Handicapped Children Act (1975), 2, 3
Public Law 99-455, Education of the Handicapped Act Amendments (1986), 3
Pull-out programs, 69

Rachlin, Jill, 4
Range of reasonableness, 88, 89
Readers' and Writers' Workshop techniques, 60

Reading
　basal readers, 64
　difficulties, 113
　language communication, 55-66
　language dysfunctions, 75-77
　language processing, 68-69
　methods, 63
　programs, 59-60, 65-66
　programs and failure, 60
　readiness, 59
　sequencing, 67-68
　strategies for slower learner, 70-71
　visual perception, 14
　visual-spatial organization, 66-67
Reading Recovery programs, 65
Receptive language, 55, 94
Referrals, 76
Regrouping, 83
Reid, Kim, 25, 45
Remembering, 16-19
Retrieval memory, 18
Risk-taking, 116
Ritchhart, Ronald, 81
Roosevelt, Franklin, 6
Rote counting, 80
Rounding, 97
Rules, information storage, 17

Sacks, Oliver, 18
Scheduling reminders, 117
School evaluations, 10
Scott-Foresman, 65
Seligson, Michelle, 30, 35
Senior, Eileen, 4
Sense of time and direction, 90
Sensory integration deficits, 8
Sensory-motor delays, 28
Sensory perception, 15, 20
Sequencing, 17, 67-68
　color coding, 68
　deficits, 30, 76, 77, 83, 93
　numeracy deficits, 98
　visual presentation, 68
Seriation, 87
Short, E. J., 38, 46
Short-term memory, 18
　deficits, 9, 29
Shyness, 26
Sight word decoding, 114

Sight words, basic, 127-28
Silver, Larry, 27, 104
Simultaneous processing, 17
Slingerland reading program, 59, 65, 66
Slow-to-warm-up child, 13
Smith, Frank, 47
Smith, Sally, 2-3
Social cues, 26
Social disabilities, 28
Social-emotional development, 27-28
Social interactions, 42
Social perceptions, 16, 20
   over-reading, 16
   under-reading, 16
Soft-sign neurological dysfunctions, 59, 70
Solomon, Bethany, 46, 48
Something's Wrong with My Child, 3
Speech dysfunctions, 57, 58
Speech therapist, 57
Speed reading, 63
Spelling difficulties, 62, 76
Standardized testing, 7-8
Stimulation problems, 26
Strategies, 10, 32, 50
   accommodating for differences, 44-48
   behavior management, 42-44
   behavior observation, 51
   caring classroom, 34-38
   for individual needs, 111-21
   language processing, 68-69
   learning process, 38-42
   problem-solving, 50, 51
   sequencing, 67-68
   for slower learner, 70-71
   visual-spatial organization, 66-67
Student-generated problem-solving, 40-41
Succeed with Math, 92
Successive processing, 17
Swanson, H. L., 38, 46

Teacher overload, 117
Teachers, 5
   accommodating various learning dysfunctions, ix
   behavior observation, 9

   continuity and stability of, 35
   education programs, 103
   general accommodations and adaptations, 109-22
   individualized approach, 37
   knowledge of early childhood development, 35
   lack of special education training, 37
   and parents, 101-8
   patience and endurance, ix
   psychological safety of, 35
Teaching
   disability, 36
   environment, 36-37
   math strategies, 92-97
   untraditional methods, 4
Temperament, 25-26
Temporal deficits, 83
Thinking aloud, 115
Thomas, A., 25
Thurston, Bill, 81
Timers and clocks, 67
Tobias, Sheila, 92
Torgesen, J. K., 46
Touch and body movement, 15
Turecki, Stanley, 3, 104

Unconventional child
   defining learning disabilities, 2-5
   recognizing, 5-10
   strategies, 10
The Unconventional Child, ix
Under-reading social interactions, 16
Uzgiris, Ina C., 56

Van Gogh, Vincent, 6
Verbal communication, 55
Verbal instructions, 20
Visual learners, 62
Visual motor weaknesses, 98
Visual orientation, 20
Visual perception, 14
   dysfunctions, 87
   reading, 14
   strategies, 65
   whole-part difficulties, 14
Visual-spatial organization weaknesses, 66-67, 76, 84, 93
Visualization techniques, 63

Wagner, Richard, 42
Weikart, David, 37
Whole child, vision of, 10
Whole language approach, 63, 64, 65
   numeracy, 85
Whole mathematics, 85
Whole-part perceptual difficulties, 14
Word families, associating, 62
Working memory, 18
Writing
   difficulties, 113
   language communication, 55-66

language dysfunctions, 75-77
language processing, 68-69
sequencing, 67-68
slower learner strategies, 70-71
visual-spatial organization, 66-67

Young Children Reinvent Arithmetic, 91

About the Author

Randy Lee Comfort is a graduate of Smith College and has a master's degree in social work and a doctorate in educational psychology. She is the director of The Learning Place, an assessment and remediation center in Denver, Colorado.

Mrs. Comfort has lived in various areas of the United States and Europe and served as a Peace Corps volunteer in Brazil. Her travels and her experiences as a mother of four children enable her to write with personal as well as professional seasoning.

Mrs. Comfort is the author of *The Unconventional Child* (self-published, 1980) and coauthor (with Constance D. Williams) of *The Child Care Catalog* (Libraries Unlimited, 1985). She has published numerous articles in professional journals and regularly presents her work at national conferences dealing with learning disabilities, education, social work, and child welfare.